CRAZY HOPE is the story of on
redeeming love. I couldn't put
vulnerability and authenticity kept wooing me into the story of God's
ability to turn ashes into beauty. If ever there's a need for Crazy Hope
it is now! Dan Moushey's book is a reminder that the God of Hope is
faithful to all generations and that He answers prayer.

— **Nancy Nelson**

Director of Donor Relations,

Warm Beach Camps and Conference Center

Bold, authentic, transparent. Through personal experience, Dan
reveals shallow and temporary voices that bind only to unveil the
One who gives "real life"—now and forever. With compassion,
Jesus observes the inmost reality of all of us, longingly seeking our
regard. Restless hearts will quickly discover their name gently
whispered, "Come... and learn of Me... and you will find rest for your
souls." He is real! Enjoy.

— **Rev. Scott Smith**

Founder of John 3:16 Good News Made Simple

In *CRAZY HOPE*, author Daniel Moushey lets his story reveal life-
changing truths which help us through the unwelcome events that
come our way. Dan's accident and subsequent events revealed his
false identity and helped him see that his true identity comes from
God alone. This perspective changed his physical handicap into an
opportunity to discover a vital relationship with God. May the Lord
use Dan and his testimony to comfort and encourage many.

— **Robert Rasmussen**

Author of *God, Get Me Through*

If you're looking for hope that's lasting and firm, Dan's raw and relatable journey shows the way. *CRAZY HOPE* exposes the flimsy ground we build our dreams and identities on, while introducing us to Solid Rock.

— **Jason Simmonds**
Director of Leadership Development
Alliance Northwest

I began reading this book and couldn't put it down. Each chapter took me deeper into Dan's life experiences. In his youth, he achieved great success and accolades which were followed by great despair and loss. Then suddenly, he encountered CRAZY HOPE. This story will take you into that discovery of hope. It is something we all need.

— **Bill Keyes**
Missionary with One Challenge International
Author of *Course of a Mentor*

It's been said that most people lead unexamined lives. Along with that, it matters greatly what viewpoint you take when you review your life story. *CRAZY HOPE* blends together a variety of perspectives (creatively using different definitions of "crazy") as Dan looks back over his life with life lessons from his experience. It is an unusual and effective way to tell your own story, invite people to reflect on their stories and introduce the Story of God. Dan's story is compelling. Youth and adults alike can benefit as Dan shows how crazy life is without Jesus!

— **Dr. Tim Roehl**
Fit & Flourish Network
Author of *Lead by Listening*

We all need crazy hope! No matter what your story or situation, you will find yourself relating to Dan's story. As you read *CRAZY HOPE,* you'll discover how to find crazy hope in your own life.

— **Dave DeVries**

Leadership Coach

CRAZY HOPE

A Journey from Losing All Hope to Finding True Hope

Daniel R. Moushey

CRAZY HOPE: A Journey from Losing All Hope to Finding True Hope

Published by Missional Challenge Publishing
www.missionalchallenge.com

Missional Challenge
PUBLISHING

ISBN 13: 978-1-952721-03-8

Manufactured in the U.S.A.

CONTENTS

Introduction.. i

Set Up.. iv

Chapter 1: A Crazy Childhood................................ 1

Chapter 2: Crazy About Baseball......................... 10

Chapter 3: Crazy About Her................................ 23

Chapter 4: A Crazy Turn of Events—From Casual to Chaos (Part I)..35

Chapter 5: A Crazy Turn of Events—From Casual to Chaos (Part II)..47

Chapter 6: Drastic Changes Make Me Crazy.................. 61

Chapter 7: Limitations Drive Me Crazy!.....................73

Chapter 8: A Crazy, Out-of-Control Life....................84

Chapter 9: A Crazy Turn of Events—From Chaos to Confusion...100

Chapter 10: Crazy Suicidal Tendencies.....................117

Chapter 11: CRAZY AWESOME HOPE.............................127

Chapter 12: Living With CRAZY HOPE..........................152

Rewriting My Chapters..187

Our True Identity..190

Our Identity in Christ..192

About the Author...197

INTRODUCTION

In May 2014, I was invited to speak at my first men's retreat. The great highlight for me was the presence of my three young adult sons and recently saved father-in-law. They knew I was planning to unveil some never-before-shared details of my life, but I think they were a little taken aback by what they heard. This book includes the stories I shared that weekend and many more. One of my reasons for writing is in response to my son's strong recommendation that I share my story. The other reason is to remind myself, as well as encourage others, about the sovereignty and love of God. God really is involved in our world. It is evident to me from personal experience and from God's word that He is living and active in all of our lives.

However, I have often failed to recognize God's hand in my life. It's hard to believe in God's sovereign love when the things we hope for don't come to pass. We often don't feel His love when we lose a job, lose a limb, or lose a loved one. In the midst of suffering and loss it's hard not to wonder if God might be against us and not for us.

Thankfully, I have learned that the opposite is true. God's sovereign love permeates every part of our lives, and His love compels Him to orchestrate events in our lives that best help wean us off the things of this world to find dependency and hope in Him alone. He has our unimaginable best in mind, wanting us to discover the fullness of who we really are in Him and the glory of being everything we are meant to be.

I have written in a way that brings you behind the scenes into my thoughts and experiences. Most of the names have been changed to protect identities. At times, my story is not pretty. Apart from God's amazing love and divine intervention, I would have suffered a shipwrecked life.

However, God is famous for bringing light out of darkness, good from evil, and resurrecting HOPE from hopelessness—and not just any hope, but a HOPE that stays anchored in the fiercest storms and keeps us afloat when all other hopes sink. There really is a CRAZY HOPE that never disappoints and makes us secure and complete in the sovereign love of God.

Therefore, having been justified by faith, we have peace with God through our Lord Jesus Christ, through whom also we have obtained our introduction by faith into this grace in which we stand; and we exult in hope of the glory of God. And not only this, but we also exult in our tribulations, knowing that tribulation brings about perseverance; and perseverance, proven character; and proven character, hope; and hope does not disappoint, because the love of God has been poured out within our hearts through the Holy Spirit who was given to us. (Romans 5:1–5)

SET UP

CRAZY

Definitions bring clarity to words; however, some words have a tendency to meander and morph in meaning over time. Take, for instance, the word "crazy." According to the Online Etymology Dictionary, it originated in the 1570s and meant "diseased or sickly." Within a decade, the definition morphed into "full of cracks or flaws." By the 1610s, crazy meandered to mean "of unsound mind, or behaving as so." The term "to drive (someone) crazy" is attested to by 1873, and by 1927, jazz circles had turned "crazy" into slang meaning "cool or exciting."[1]

It's crazy how many ways the word crazy can be used today. According to various dictionaries, crazy has over fifteen different definitions. I have chosen the

---

[1] Online Etymology Dictionary, s.v. "crazy," accessed December 11, 2020, https://www.etymonline.com/word/crazy.

eleven definitions that best describe the first half of my life's journey as the chapter titles for this book. Ending each chapter is a Crazy Contemplation that is meant to challenge, encourage, and inspire. My hope and prayer is that God will use *CRAZY HOPE* to bring healing and new perspective into your life.

CRAZY:

1. senseless; impractical; unsound:
A Crazy Childhood

2. intensely enthusiastic; passionately excited:
Crazy About Baseball

3. very enamored or infatuated (usually followed by *about*):
Crazy About Her

4. appearing absurdly out of place:
A Crazy Turn of Events—From Casual to Chaos (Part I)

5. appearing absurdly out of place:
A Crazy Turn of Events—From Casual to Chaos (Part II)

6. intensely anxious or eager; impatient:

Drastic Changes Make Me Crazy

7. extremely annoyed or angry:

Limitations Drive Me Crazy!

8. *Slang*. with great speed or recklessness:

A Crazy, Out-of-Control Life

9. unusual; bizarre:

A Crazy Turn of Events—From Chaos to Confusion

10. mentally insane; demented:

Crazy Suicidal Tendencies

11. wonderful; excellent; perfect:

CRAZY AWESOME HOPE!

12. *Slang*. with great enthusiasm or energy; to an extreme:

Living with CRAZY HOPE

HOPE

The second word in the title is Hope. The Greek words for hope, *elpízō* and *elpís*, contain two main ingredients. *Elpízō*: to expect with desire. *Elpís*: desire of some good with expectation of obtaining it.[2] In short, hope is "desired expectation."

In its very essence, the word hope can be a problematic, unpredictable and even dangerous concept for one simple reason: our desired expectations often fall through. Consequently, hope can be somewhat of a gamble!

Gamblers place their bets with great desire and expectation that someday they will hit the jackpot; however, few win. Hope can be extremely risky because of the equation: great desire + great expectation = great disappointment.

I have witnessed many people, including myself, fall into despair when hope was dashed against the rocks. This can lead a person to a place they never thought possible—hopelessness. It is not uncommon for bitterness, anger, disillusionment, clinical depression, mental illness, or suicide to follow close behind. So what's the answer?

---

[2] Spiros Zodhiates, *The Complete Word Study Dictionary: New Testament* (Chattanooga: AMG Publishers, 2000), s.v. "Elpizo", "Elpis", Logos Bible Software.

Is it possible to embrace our desires while eliminating all expectations? Or, like a Buddhist monk, should we seek the extermination of our desires until we reach nirvana? It's interesting to note that nirvana is more a state of mind than it is a place—it is an altered state of consciousness. In fact, the Sanskrit word *nirvana* literally means "to blow out, to be extinguished." Once all desire is eliminated, so is all expectation. This forms another possible equation: zero desires + zero expectations = zero consciousness.

Sounds a little extreme until you consider the millions of people around the world who are checking out of life by means of drug and alcohol abuse. You don't have to belong to a monastery to learn how to grow numb to life. I know I've tried. When a person has suffered great loss and all hope seems gone, they will do the craziest things just to survive. Unfortunately, the extinction of one's self, whether mentally or physically, is a very real option.

There is a flip side. Maybe you have experienced the opposite to be true—all your desired expectations have been obtained. You've achieved all that you ever hoped for. You attended your school of choice and have your dream career. Your spouse is wonderful; your family is perfect; your house is pristine; your neighbors are gracious; and all your investments are up. You even pick the jackpot numbers to win the Powerball lottery!

You've reaped everything there is to gain except one thing: contentment. It is a terrifying thing to discover that after you have obtained every desired expectation, in the end, it all seems meaningless. Just ask the writer of Ecclesiastes. King Solomon not only had it all, he did it all. He spent years searching and experimenting only to come to the bitter conclusion, *"Vanity of vanities, all is vanity!"* (Ecclesiastes 1:2).

This forms another possible equation: all desires + all expectations = meaninglessness.

Thankfully, CRAZY HOPE has one final equation: Eternal Desires + Eternal Expectations = Eternal Completeness. True CRAZY HOPE comes from God alone. It is the only HOPE that transcends this present universe and is not limited by our failed efforts or the flawed failures of others. It is the only HOPE that has carried me through the hardest of times and given me the proper perspective in the best of times. The rest of this book unfolds my difficult journey to discover life's greatest blessing... CRAZY HOPE.

However, before discovering CRAZY HOPE, I had to endure the loss of every earthly hope. Not only did this leave me wounded, scarred, and broken, but it also caused an identity crisis. Since then I have discovered a profound truth: our greatest hope forms our identity. If our greatest hope fails, then our identity is in jeopardy.

Sometimes we can place our hope in the craziest things—but depending on your definition of "crazy," that just might not be a bad thing.

CHAPTER 1

senseless; impractical; totally unsound:
A Crazy Childhood

If you grew up in a small town, you know how word gets around. Everyone seems to know a little something about everyone. Whether or not it is accurate is often beside the point. Unfortunately, a lot of people know a little something about Granite Falls, Washington.

If you've heard of Granite Falls, you might think of logging trucks and taverns, bikers and hikers, drugs and thugs. Or you may have read the Rolling Stone Magazine article that mentioned Granite Falls being nicknamed "Methville" or "Cranktown" by some in the community. Whatever you might have heard, it may not be entirely accurate.

In spite of its flaws, Granite Falls has its charm and appeal. I know Granite Falls as a quaint little town strategically nestled up against the picture perfect

Mount Pilchuck. It's changed in many ways over the years. Some of the most charming, loving, hospitable and helpful people I know live in Granite Falls. It is a place where the community still functions like a community—neighbor helping neighbor, patrons willing to spend a little more to support their local businesses. As for appeal, no one can deny the beautiful landscape that surrounds the town, lending an alluring invitation to all avid hikers, fishers, campers, and bicycle enthusiasts.

I did, however, have a life before Granite Falls. For the first six weeks of my life, I lived in an adoption agency in Bremerton, WA. The name given to me at that time was Joseph. Not wishing to name me after my adoptive father's brother, Uncle Joe, my adoptive parents decided to name me Daniel Ryan.

My mother called me Danny and so did everyone else. This was unfortunate because it did not take long for the kids in elementary school to figure out that my name rhymed with a particular part of the human anatomy. The "Name Song" was brutal on my little ego, as the children sang with glee, "Danny Danny fo fanny..." I can still hear the song echoing in my mind.

The kids called me fat, but my mom reassured me that I was husky. I wasn't certain who to believe. Call it what you will—solid, dense, thick, heavy, or husky—to kids in elementary school, it's fat.

My younger years were filled with children, lots and lots of children. My mother single-handedly ran a daycare out of our home from 1969-1985. You could say that I went from adoption care straight into childcare. She was licensed to oversee six full-time and six part-time children. I both loved and hated it. On one hand, there was always someone who would push toy cars around in the dirt with me. On the other hand, there was always someone to push toy cars around in the dirt with me. Sometimes I wished it was just me and my family, but then again, my brother and sister weren't much for playing with toy cars in the dirt.

My mother was a pretty resilient lady to say the least. However, if she hadn't had multiple opportunities to escape into one of her many romance novels throughout the day, I don't think even she would have endured those years.

My dad also worked with children as a social worker at the Department of Social Health Services (DSHS) in

Everett, WA. I didn't really understand what he did at his job. All I knew was he didn't have much energy for playing when he got home. His favorite pastime was to lay down on the couch in a private room while smoking his tobacco pipe. I now understand why. My dad saw and experienced a lot of difficult domestic violence situations at work. If that wasn't hard enough, he also had the weight of responsibility to determine whether or not a child should be removed from an abusive home. He never talked about his work.

My dad did like to talk about the day he would finally retire. It was one of the only subjects that seemed to breathe new life into him. He would go on and on about his hope and dream of someday opening up an ice cream and candy shop in town. However, retirement didn't unfold in the manner he would have ever desired or expected.

The Roman Catholic Church played a key role in my dad's life, but I'm not sure how religion helped him. It seemed to bring more discouragement than anything, and he was motivated by fear, not faith. As a staunch Roman Catholic, he saw it as his duty to drag us kids to church every Sunday morning. We would ask, "Why do we have to go to church?"

Dad's answer was always the same, "You have to go to the Roman Catholic Church in order to go to heaven." This "heavenly package" included infant baptism, regular church attendance, confession, catechism, and communion.

To help accommodate for his children's lack of desire, my dad allowed my brother and I to climb the narrow wooden stairs of the church and sit in the tiny balcony. In my six-year-old mind, the only perk I could find was a long fly strip dangling from the ceiling that was always covered with flies. That could hold my attention for a period of time, but even the fly strip was not enough motivation to come back week after week.

Dad eventually talked us into becoming altar boys, which also had some perks. We were given five dollars a month, a white robe, the privilege of sitting on stage, and the power to light candles with real fire. The best part, though, was that we were allowed to enter the back room behind the platform and eat the leftover wafers, and there were always two fly strips!

Having his sons become altar boys did give my dad a sense of accomplishment; but it did not release him from his fear, anger and bondage. Something continued to gnaw at him, and it took a toll as time went on.

My elementary school years can be summed up in one word: average. Certainly nothing to write home about. I was teased along with most other kids, and since I was always on the chunky side, I picked up the nickname "moo-cow" derived from my last name, Moushey. However, by fifth grade, something began developing that gave me an edge and helped shape the direction of my future. Muscles!

For some reason, I was gifted with muscular thighs and a strong upper body. To this day, most people assume I lift weights and work out, although this is not the case. Fortunately for me, along with some athleticism, I was blessed to have classmates who were also great athletes. The four of us knew how to play well together, and our personal rivalries with one another sharpened and strengthened our skills.

Every recess from fourth to sixth grade, the competition was fierce. Grant and I always formed a team, and Taylor always teamed up with Ryan. The role of team captain rotated between the four of us, but the same rivalry always formed. It seemed strange whenever Grant found himself on Taylor's team or Ryan on mine. This special rivalry pushed us to excel, especially when springtime arrived.

Crazy Contemplation:

In our younger years, life can seem a little crazy—"senseless; impractical; and totally unsound." Perhaps it's because we are just trying to figure things out. What makes life even more confusing are the nicknames we often acquire. Whether assigned to a small town nestled up against a mountain or a five-year-old nestled up in their mother's arms, degrading nicknames have a way of undermining the essence of who we truly are.

Hurtful nicknames are also some of the first lies we start believing about ourselves. They often begin forming our first false sense of identity. "If I weren't so fat, ugly, slow, clumsy, short, tall, or stupid, maybe I would be more acceptable."

This is one of the tactics the evil one uses as well. He whispers in our ear, "You're unlovable, worthless, alone, undesirable, foolish, guilty, and hopeless." He excels at taking the insults we receive from others and magnifying them in our thoughts. He knows that when we hear a lie long enough, we will start to believe it.

7

At the time, I didn't realize that my identity was being formed. The situations we experience in the past not only influence the present, but they can obscure how we view the future in ways we can't fully comprehend. If we are not careful, we can allow the past to define us. The lie I have always struggled with is, "You are a burden and unacceptable."

Although I was adopted, my dad and mom never treated me any different. I never experienced abuse or anything tragic. Life just seemed normal.

However, in the back of my mind, I always wondered why my birth father or mother gave me away. Was I a burden? Was I unacceptable to them? Was it their desire to give me away or were they reluctant? Did they have a choice or were they forced? Did they care about me or could they not care less? Did they ever want me? Did they ever have the desire to hold me, to meet me, or even see me? Do they ever wonder where or who I am?

I may never get answers to my questions, but they do raise a profound thought... *our origin matters*. Whether we realize it or not, our parents give us our first impression of who God is and what He is like. So, if our parents were distant, maybe that's why we think

God is distant. If our parents didn't care, why would God care? If our parents gave us away, why would God want us back?

These questions can lay dormant and undetected in the core of our soul for years; and if we are not careful, they can lead us to believe the most pernicious lie of all: God cannot be trusted. If God can't be trusted, then our greatest hope will be placed in something else—something false, something tied to this world, something counterfeit. If our greatest hope is not in God, then our identity will also be false, tied to this world, and counterfeit.

However, God has a new name He wants to give each of us—a name that coincides with our true, eternal identity. He grants it to us once we are willing to abandon the lies we believe. Jesus said it this way: *"The truth will make [set] you free... So if the Son makes you free, you will be free indeed"* (John 8:32, 36).

Jesus offers us our true identity, one that says, "You're loved, precious, never alone, desirable, redeemed, justified, and eternally hopeful."

We must decide whose voice we will choose to listen to and believe.

CHAPTER 2

intensely enthusiastic; passionately excited:
Crazy About Baseball

Spring has a way of quickening our senses. Feeling the warm forgotten sun bursting through the clouds, smelling flowers and freshly cut grass, seeing people tending to their yards, hearing dogs barking and people laughing, and tasting bubble gum in my mouth—these are my memories of riding my bike to the Little League field.

I loved Little League! Not because I was good—in fact, my first year was a total disaster. Little League had a great impact on me for one reason: Tim Brogan. Coach Brogan believed in me. He knew how to bring out the best in everyone. As a result, I didn't stay in right field very long.

By my third and final year in Little League, Coach Brogan had made me into a pretty good first baseman.

Back in those days, Granite Falls only had one Little League team, and with Coach Brogan's help, we made it to the championship our final year.

The championship game was a nail-biter. The team we were playing had a well-developed squeeze play. Whenever there was a runner on third base, the batter would bunt the ball down the first base line in order to advance the runner home. They had already executed this play three or four times during the game. Every time the ball was bunted, I would sprint up the first base line, grab the ball, tag the batter and throw out the runner scoring from third. Double play!

I don't know if it was deliberate, but the final time they ran the squeeze play, the runner bunting the ball plowed into me, nearly knocking me out cold. The assistant coach ran out onto the field to assess my condition. Holding up two fingers, he asked, "Danny, how many fingers do I have up?"

I answered, "Three... I mean two." Thankfully, he had the compassion and foresight to keep me in the game.

Things were going well until the bottom half of the seventh and final inning. We were ahead by one run. Our best pitcher, Taylor, was on the mound. Ryan was at third, Grant at second, and I was at first base. We only needed one final out to win the game—but then it happened.

Taylor started to grow weary and began walking batters. When the bases were loaded, Coach Brogan called a time out. He ran out to the pitcher's mound and motioned me over. Then he did something very unexpected. Coach Brogan placed the ball in my glove and said, "Danny, I just want you to throw strikes."

I couldn't believe what I was being asked to do! I swallowed hard, trying to dislodge the lump in my throat. There was a huge problem running through my twelve-year-old baseball-capped head: I had never pitched in a game before... ever!

Taylor headed to first base, and I stood on the pitcher's mound in a state of shock. "How did I get into this position?" I wondered as children, parents, and grandparents looked on and cheered from the stands.

With the sound of cowbells clanging in the background, I took a quick look at the team and saw Taylor, Grant, and Ryan cheering me on from the infield. Win or lose, we were in this together.

After I threw a few warm-up pitches, the umpire was ready. "Play Ball!"

On the mound, I saw the catcher point one finger to the ground. "I guess he wants me to throw a fastball?" I thought.

Since I had no other pitch in my arsenal, I wound up and threw the ball directly over home plate. "Strike two!"

"Hey! I can do this!" I thought to myself as the catcher threw the ball back. Once again, I reared back and threw another fastball over the plate. This time, the batter swung! The ground ball came right back at me. I quickly bent over, scooped up the ball, and threw the runner out at first. We were Little League champions!

This was my first adrenaline-producing, game-winning encounter, and I thrived in the moment. I would readily meet this challenge time and again for the next few years. There seemed to be something in my DNA that excelled when the pressure to perform was placed on my shoulders. I only wished that my parents would have been there. I think they would have been proud of me.

That year, all four of us—Taylor, Grant, Ryan, and I—were chosen to join the Snohomish All-Star Team. Our team did well, but we fell short of making it to the Little League Baseball World Series held each year in Williamsport, Pennsylvania. However, I received an accolade after our final all-star game that I still cherish to this day.

The all-star coach gathered our team together and gave one final speech before we parted ways to enjoy the rest of the summer. As we sat sorrowful with our heads bowed low, plucking blades of grass with our fingertips, the coach stood and spoke these parting words: "You guys have nothing to be ashamed of. You played well this year! To me, you are all all-stars; but if there is one all-star among you, it's Danny Moushey."

"What?" I thought. "Did he really just say what I think he said? All-Star of the all-stars!"

I still do not fully understand why the coach singled me out, but I believe it was a gift. It strengthened my resolve to pour all of my energy and effort into striving after a professional baseball career. In other words, my greatest hope and all of my desires and expectations were strategically placed in the one thing that gave me my sense of belonging and purpose.

As time progressed, baseball became my all-encompassing passion and pursuit. It was where I received encouragement and honor, community and family, and where I felt welcomed and wanted. *Baseball formed my identity*. I vowed that nothing was going to stop me from making my dream into reality.

But not everyone believed pro-baseball was in my future. Time and again I endured my dad's great negativity, "Danny, you'll never make it. There is a one-in-a-million chance that you will ever make it to the big leagues!"

Deep down, I knew my dad was only trying to protect me. He knew firsthand the great disappointment shattered hopes can bring. But my response was always the same, "One in a million? Then I will be the one!"

During middle school, I discovered two very important things: girls and speed. There were three girls named Kim that liked me, but there was only one I wanted to be with. The only problem was that she was a year ahead of me. I dated Kim Haverfield for two weeks.

I don't remember much from middle school, but I do remember those two weeks.

There was something I really liked about Kim—actually there were a lot of things I liked about her—but I knew it wouldn't last. Soon, I would be moving up to eighth grade at the middle school, and Kim would start her freshman year at the high school a couple blocks away. I could only hope that once I made it to high school, maybe—just maybe—we could continue where we left off.

The second thing I discovered in middle school was my speed. I was the fastest runner in my class. I loved sprinting drills during basketball practice, especially running lines. This exercise consisted of the team lining up on one side of the gym and sprinting back and forth to touch each line laid out on the court, marking off the quarter, half, three-quarter, and full court lines. The coaches always watched to see who would win. I thrived in that kind of environment. With strong, muscular thighs, I was explosive from the start of a sprint. By the end of middle school, I could almost dunk a basketball with only a five-foot-nine-inch frame.

When springtime arrived in my freshman year of high school, I tried out for the Granite Falls Tigers baseball team along with Grant, Taylor, and Ryan. Both Taylor and I were selected as starters for the varsity team. Taylor hit in the leadoff position, and I was placed second in the batting order and played first base.

My brother Brian played shortstop and was pretty good at it. He was a couple years older than me and in his junior year. Brian managed to earn the nickname "The Vacuum Cleaner" because he was great at fielding a ground ball, just not so good at throwing the ball accurately to first base. I definitely earned the letter on my jacket that year as I saved his bacon time and again by stretching, jumping, diving, and digging out balls thrown in the dirt to first base.

You could always tell who I was from a distance—I was the guy covered in dirt. I guess I owe Brian. Without his help, the coaches would never have known what I was capable of doing!

The Tigers had an opportunity to make it to the playoffs my freshman year; and once again, in the most important game of the season, I was thrust into an adrenaline-producing, game-winning situation.

This time, the game was tied, there were two outs, and it was the bottom half of the ninth inning. It looked like we would have to go to extra innings. I stepped into the batter's box and quickly got my signals from the coach. He had already told me that he just wanted me to get on base, so it wasn't a surprise when I got the sign to lay down a bunt.

I gently bunted the ball down the third base line and beat out the throw. Now on first base, I saw the third base coach give me the sign to steal second base. The pitcher went from a slow wind up to a quick release stretch. It didn't matter. I had been given the green light, and I was ready to launch.

In my mind, I was Ricky Henderson from the Oakland A's, arguably the greatest leadoff hitter of all time. He was my role model. I remember the game where he broke the record for all-time steals. After diving headfirst into second base, he ripped the base out of the ground and lifted it over his head. I still have a plaque and signed ball commemorating Henderson's incredible, unbeatable feat. I had perfected my stance, takeoff, sprint, and head-first slide from hours of mimicking this baseball legend. So, when I took off to steal second base, it was Danny empowered with the spirit of Ricky.

However, both the pitcher and the catcher knew exactly what I intended to do. Not appreciating the size of my lead off first base, the pitcher kept throwing the ball to first base to keep me close to the bag.

On the next pitch, I took off like a shot! Unbeknownst to me, the catcher had signaled the pitcher to throw a pitch out, allowing him to make an easy throw to second. With tensions running high, the catcher threw a wild ball to second base, sending it into the outfield and allowing me to advance safely to third. The Granite Falls grandstands erupted as the momentum grew!

No longer under the threat of base runners stealing, the pitcher went back into his long wind up. While Grant stepped back into the batter's box, the third base coach leaned in and whispered in my ear, "Danny, check out the pitcher's wind up. Do you think you can beat his throw and steal home for the win?"

Although I had never stolen home before, after observing the next pitch, I was convinced I could do it! My adrenaline surged as I watched the catcher toss the ball back to the mound.

The pitcher took a quick look at me and started his long wind up. The third base coach leaned in to give me instructions, but I was already gone and heading for home.

As the ball crossed over the plate, three things happened simultaneously. With no understanding of what was happening, Grant took a swing at the ball; the catcher caught the ball; and I slid head-first into home just before the tag and just under Grant's swinging bat! The umpire called, "SAFE!!" and we were headed to the playoffs!

That year I was nominated all-varsity first baseman. With a couple freshman starters on the varsity team, word got around that college and pro scouts were starting to observe our performance. My dream of playing professional baseball seemed closer than ever.

Crazy Contemplation:

There is a reason I placed crazy—"intensely enthusiastic; passionately excited"—hope in baseball: it formed my identity. Baseball gave me a sense of worth and value. It's bizarre how catching and throwing a little white ball and hitting it with a stick can produce feelings of meaning and purpose; however, that's all they are—feelings.

Feelings come and feelings go. Health is good one day and declines the next. Skills sharpen and they diminish. Talent peaks and talent fades.

But there is something deeper here. *Anytime our identity stems from something we do, it's only a matter of time before an identity crisis occurs.* There will eventually be a day when our doing is done. There will inevitably come a day when our performance subsides.

Whether it is an accident, a sickness, a disability, a divorce, a job layoff; or whether life changes and our children move out, retirement comes, we move into a care facility, and our friends die—none of it is stable. Nothing is permanent.

The point is this: identity that does not transcend doing will inadvertently become bound to it. As a result, when we can no longer do, we will become disillusioned.

Our *true* identity, on the other hand—who we really are—has nothing to do with what we do or don't do. Unfortunately, we live in a culture that believes otherwise. We are wired to think an awful lot about doing. Consider how the conversation goes when you meet someone for the first time. We often lead with the question, "What do you *do* for a living?" Why do we ask this? It would be interesting to take a poll. I wonder if the question has less to do with curiosity about how someone earns a paycheck and more with trying to discern the identity of the other person by learning what they do. At any rate, I am grateful that we still label ourselves "human beings" rather than "human doings."

Here are a few questions to ponder when considering identity:

- If you were incapable of doing anything, would your identity be threatened?
- If you were incapable of doing anything, how would you identify yourself?
- Who are you, really?

It is impossible to discover your true identity without answering the following questions. Your true identity starts with your origin:

Who created you?

Why did He create you?

To whom do you belong?

CHAPTER 3

very enamored or infatuated
(usually followed by about):
Crazy About Her

The summer following my freshman year of high school brought some of the best and worst moments of my life. As baseball season ended, another kind of season began. In my fifteen-year-old body and mind, the season of love was about to blossom as I grew in fascination and appreciation for the incredible and unique ways the opposite sex was designed. The different ways they looked, walked, talked, dressed, smiled, smelled, laughed, giggled and grinned—especially Sarah Houston.

Sarah was a year older than I was and heading into her junior year of high school. She had long, dark brown hair, beautiful eyes, and a smile that made me melt. But even more, Sarah had a way of making me feel alive. I never knew a girl could be so fun.

My best friends at the time, Henry and Toby, didn't know what to think. It was a tough time for them. For the longest time, we had been like the three musketeers. We did everything together. It was always, "All for one and one for all!" But now, our allegiance was being tested.

On one hand, they envied my relationship with Sarah. They wanted a "Sarah" in their lives too. On the other hand, Sarah brought along friends—friends of the female persuasion. All that to say, it didn't take long for Henry and Toby to start warming up to the idea that Dan having a girlfriend might not be such a bad thing after all.

That summer, Sarah and I got very close. We were inseparable; all I wanted was to be with her. We would talk on the phone for hours. Any chance I got, I rode my bike for miles just to be with her. Once Sarah got her driver's license, things got even better. Now we had more freedom, more privacy, and more possibilities.

One moonlit night, Sarah and I snuck out and drove to Kayak Point together. We sat on the beach and talked for hours about our dreams, our disappointments, our hopes, fears, and longings. We swam together in the moonlight. I never wanted the night to end.

It all seemed so perfect. No one had ever taken so much interest in my life before, and I began to wonder if she could be the one. Sarah really cared, and I found myself falling in love with her.

At the beginning of August, I began getting into shape for football practice. I started lifting weights and began jogging a mile or two a day. The only thing was that I hated long-distance running. When I signed up for cross-country in middle school, it was one of the biggest mistakes of my life. Sprinting a hundred yards is one thing; running five miles is quite another.

I totally identified with Gimli the dwarf from *The Lord of the Rings* when he said, "I'm wasted on cross-country! We dwarves are natural sprinters! Very dangerous over short distances!" Apparently, the varsity football coach agreed with Gimli.

During the first week of football practice, Coach Ethans noticed my increased speed and the additional strength I had gained over the past year. One day after practice, he came to tell me what he had been thinking:

"Danny, I want to create a new position this year. We have never had a slotback, and I was wondering if you would be interested in playing the position?"

For the football illiterate, a slotback is a cross between a running back and a receiver. If there was ever a position I would have handpicked for myself, this was it. Now it was being offered to me, so I trained even harder.

During the last weekend of summer break, a strange thing happened that I will never forget. As I begrudgingly started out on another two-mile run, I could tell something was different. As I was approaching home, to my great surprise, I found that I had even more energy than when I started! So I kept going. I ran to the other side of town and back. Again, I wasn't even winded.

I then took off in an all-out sprint, running back and forth across town, zigzagging down alleyways and cross streets, trying to wear myself out; but I couldn't do it. As darkness began to fall, I finally gave up trying. It was the most incredible experience! I wasn't sure what was happening—all I knew was that I liked it!

On Friday, August 29, 1986, we were two weeks into football practice. Granite Falls had been experiencing a drought for the past few months; but on that day, it finally started to rain. It was refreshing.

After practice, Henry and I made arrangements with Sarah and her friend Jessica to drive into Everett. Our plans weren't extravagant. We were just going to bum around town. Any reason to get together with Sarah would have sufficed.

Being gentlemen, Henry and I piled into the cramped back seat of the little Honda Civic. Jessica sat in the passenger seat in front of me. I jokingly fastened the seatbelt across my waist and cinched it down tight while teasing Sarah, "You can never be too safe when riding with a new driver!"

At dusk, we finally made our way back onto the infamous Crooked Mile Road, the main road in and out of Granite Falls at the time. Henry and I began blowing up some paper lunch sacks we had found on the floor. For laughs, we popped them, pretending like the tires were blowing out. We laughed and kidded around with each other. I loved watching Sarah smile.

As we came up on the last curve in the road, our carousing turned into chaotic screams. Calamity forced its way in as two bright headlights rushed headlong into our lives. In an instant, our lives were forever changed...

Tragedy erupts

Darkness interrupts

Chaos forced its throng

Bright lights rush headlong

Corrupting our song.

Tears and fears prolong

Summertime is gone.

Crazy Contemplation:

At fifteen years of age, I possessed two crazy, "very enamored or infatuated" hopes that formed my identity. Baseball filled my need to be accepted, and Sarah filled my need to be loved. As long as I possessed these two hopes, my life seemed complete. They fulfilled my desire for belonging.

In reality, however, only two types of hope exist: false temporal hope and true everlasting hope. Crazy false hope is placing one's greatest desire and expectation in something finite and limited. This could be a person, a thing, an idea, a condition, or some accomplishment that is confined to this world. We can place our greatest hope in anything:

- A person: a girlfriend or boyfriend, a spouse, a child, a parent, a friendship, a teacher, a boss, etc.
- A thing: a home, a school, an occupation, a car, a boat, technology, etc.
- A condition: health, wealth, popularity, peace, reconciliation, being understood, etc.
- An idea: to be married, become a parent, have a career, future retirement, etc.
- An accomplishment: being a professional, becoming famous, being self-sufficient, gaining worldly success, etc.

Whether crazy false hope is obtained or not, it always leaves us incomplete. It cannot satisfy because it was never designed to make us whole. At its best, crazy false hope provides a false sense of belonging and becomes a great distraction. At its worst, it becomes an agent of destruction and great disappointment.

In the end, crazy false hope has no ability to save our souls. Compared to the real deal, it is a counterfeit that offers false answers to our questions about life's purpose and meaning. However, the real tragedy is this: when we hold tightly to crazy false hope, it prevents us from receiving true everlasting hope.

I once heard a story at a conference that has stuck with me ever since. It's about a little girl who loved pearl necklaces. One day, when passing by a vending machine, the little girl asked her daddy for twenty-five cents to purchase a plastic pearl necklace. The little girl's daddy gladly obliged, and with great joy she ran to the vending machine, inserted the quarter, and turned the handle. Out came her treasured necklace. She quickly put it on and never took it off.

Two weeks later, Daddy walked into her bedroom to tuck her in for the night. Sitting at the foot of her bed, Daddy saw his daughter's necklace, now tattered and faded, and asked, "Sweetie, can Daddy have your necklace?"

The little girl opened her eyes wide and quickly placed her hands over the necklace. She replied, "Daddy... no, Daddy, I love my pearl necklace."

Daddy got up, leaned in and kissed his daughter goodnight, and spoke softly, "Alright honey, you can keep your necklace. I love you."

The next night, Daddy came in and repeated the process. This time, however, when he sat down at the foot of her bed, the little girl quickly grabbed her stuffed teddy bear and held it tightly against her chest, hiding her necklace. Daddy asked again, "Sweetie, can Daddy have your necklace?"

"Oh Daddy, not my necklace," she answered. Then, with a smile, she offered a compromise, "But you can have my teddy bear."

Daddy was patient, "No honey, I want your necklace. You keep your teddy bear." Daddy got up, kissed his little girl, and said, "I love you. Goodnight."

A week later, Daddy was walking by his little girl's bedroom and heard her crying. He quickly entered to see what was wrong and found his little girl sitting up in the middle of her bed with her hands in her lap holding her necklace.

Teary-eyed, the little girl stretched out her hands towards Daddy with her palms up and slowly released her grip on her favorite treasure. As tears rolled down her cheeks, she said, "Daddy, I want to give you my necklace."

Overjoyed, Daddy sat down next to his daughter, lifted the faded and tattered necklace out of her hands, and placed it in his pocket. He said, "Sweetie, Daddy has been waiting for you to give me your necklace."

While he was speaking, he reached into his other pocket and pulled out a velvet-lined box. As he lifted the lid, the little girl's eyes grew as big as saucers. With great joy, Daddy said, "Now I can give you my grandmother's pearl necklace."

As he clasped the necklace around his daughter's neck, he spoke softly into her ear, "Daddy has been waiting for you to give up what was fading and worthless, so I could give you something unfading and priceless."

The little girl cherished the pearl necklace for the rest of her life. Its beauty never faded and it became more valuable with each passing day. The necklace taught the little girl that Daddy was trustworthy and that when he asked for something she treasured, it was only to replace it with something greater.

Do you have a twenty-five cent necklace in your life? Something you're protecting and holding onto tightly? Something that attempts to fill a need you believe nothing else will satisfy? Something that is preventing you from receiving the priceless gift of eternal life and hope our Father in Heaven is waiting to give you? Jesus said,

> *"The kingdom of heaven is like a treasure hidden in the field, which a man found and hid again; and from joy over it he goes and sells all that he has and buys that field." (Matthew 13:44).*

Could there really be such a treasure? A treasure that, upon discovering it, we would gladly give up all that we have to possess? I know there is because once I discovered it, I was never the same. Not only did I find the treasure, but my true identity was found there as well.

If our greatest hope does not have God and what He has done for us as its foundation, we will never discover our true identity.

Unfortunately, it would be a few more years before I exhausted all my crazy false hopes. I would have to step on a few more false hope land mines before I found the field with the treasure. I could have never imagined that the following chapters would one day be part of my life story.

CHAPTER 4

appearing absurdly out of place:
A Crazy Turn of Events—from Casual to Chaos

Part 1

Like waking up from a nap, I began to regain consciousness. Hunched over, I slowly lifted my head and cracked open my eyelids. It was dark and eerily quiet. I was dazed and confused and wondered if I was still dreaming.

My surroundings were unrecognizable. It appeared I was in the backseat of a car, but it was deformed and mangled. The smell of gasoline and oil filled the air. "This has to be a nightmare," I muttered.

A passing beam of light from outside the vehicle momentarily lit up my surroundings, allowing me to make out the silhouette of a young girl in front of me. She sat motionless. "Sarah?" I thought.

I tried propping myself up with my left hand but was unsuccessful. I reached out with my right to touch her right shoulder. "Sarah," I asked, "is that you?" No response.

Determined to get her attention, I entangled my fingers in her soft brown hair and gently tugged. "Sarah! Is that you? Are you alright?" Silence.

Henry suddenly woke up and screamed, "Aww! Get off my leg!" Unbeknownst to me, I was hunched over on Henry's right leg, using it for leverage and support. Again, the interior of the car was lit up by headlight beams as vehicles started surrounding us. Blood gushed from Henry's mouth, soaking his clothes. His front teeth were gone, shattered from the impact.

Then a terrifying noise, like a jackhammer, pierced our ears. Henry screamed again with a blood-garbled lisp, "Get off my leg!!" I tried, but I couldn't. All my efforts seemed to make matters worse. I felt like I was in a vice, constricted and bound up in a bent over position. I tried to unbuckle my seatbelt, but it was wedged into my abdomen. My hope of this being a bad dream started to fade.

Muffled voices came from outside the vehicle as people scurried and scrambled around the car. My nightmare became reality when the door on my side was cut through and snapped open.

A Granite Falls fireman quickly explained the situation. "You have been in a severe head-on collision. We are cutting the car apart to extract you from the automobile." I flashed back to the last thing I remembered. Two bright lights, then darkness.

The fireman tried to unbuckle my seatbelt but was unsuccessful. He pulled out a knife and cut through the belt. As the tension was released, I was shocked to discover that I had no feeling in my left leg! Quickly and methodically, he began to pull me from the wreckage. I tried to help him, but I was too weak.

I was placed on a gurney and immediately rushed to a nearby ambulance. On the way, I caught a glimpse of the chaotic accident scene. Lights and sirens flooded the area as people rushed around with flashlights. Police cars, fire trucks, ambulances, and loud generators surrounded two crushed vehicles. One generator supplied power to the extraction tool called the "jaws of life." I watched as it continued to cut through the Honda Civic like it was a tin can.

My mind began to race as they lifted me into the ambulance. What was wrong with me? What about my friends? Why wasn't Sarah moving? Was she alive?

Inside the ambulance it was well lit. I looked down at my peach tank top covered in blood. "Where did all this blood come from?" I asked the paramedic.

"You have a deep gash on your forehead," he said. "Just try to relax." But I couldn't relax; something was terribly wrong.

Greatly concerned, I stated as clearly as I could, "I CANNOT FEEL MY LEFT LEG!"

The same reply was given, "Just try to relax and stay calm."

We quickly arrived at the hospital and I was transported straight to the emergency room. My dad and mom arrived soon after. The minute they saw me, the color drained from their faces.

I was rushed down the hall into another room where all my clothes were cut off and I was prepped for surgery. The last thing I remember is staring into another set of bright lights. This time, they loomed overhead as I tried to lay still while shivering on the operating table.

I can't imagine what each of our parents felt that night. How do you explain feeling helplessness, horror, concern, anger, confusion and compassion all at the same time?

I was in surgery for many hours that night. Periodically, my parents received vaguely negative updates. Finally, the surgeon stepped out and prepared them for the worst: "Danny has suffered a lot of internal bleeding and damage to his midsection. We are doing everything we can to save him. Now we'll have to wait and see if he makes it."

My dad fainted upon hearing the news and was admitted a couple rooms down from me, leaving my mom all alone.

My injuries were numerous and more would be discovered in the weeks ahead. For now, in addition to the gash on my forehead, the surgeon had discovered internal damage and bleeding resulting from the lap seatbelt I had been wearing. A main artery in my lower stomach was crushed along with a portion of my intestinal tract. My kidneys had shut down, and my lungs were filling with water.

After two long days of sedation, I finally woke up in the intensive care unit. I quickly recognized I was in a hospital; what I didn't recognize were all the tubes exiting my body and the machines to which they were attached.

My dad, who had just been released, is the first person I remember seeing. He had a big grin on his face as he sat in a chair right next to my bed. As soon as I could speak, I asked him the question that was burning in my heart, "Will I be able to play baseball?"

His answer was vague, "I hope so, Danny."

As I pulled back the covers, I discovered a number of changes to my body. There was a long incision extending from my sternum to my pubic bone. It looked as if someone had thrust me open with a Samurai sword, then stapled me back together. Due to the size and location of this enormous incision, my belly button was no longer in the same spot.

The surgeon explained, "Danny, you had a lot of internal bleeding, so we had to open you up. You suffered quite a bit of damage from the lap belt you were wearing."

The next thing I noticed was a plastic bag hanging off the left side of my abdomen just below my rib cage. "That is a colostomy bag," the surgeon told me. "Six feet of your intestine were crushed and needed to be extracted. For now, you will have bowel movements in this bag. Depending on how everything heals, it may be temporary or it could be permanent."

The third thing I noticed was another long incision, stapled together, extending from the top of my inner right thigh to the inside of my right knee. The surgeon continued, "We had to use a healthy main artery from your right leg to replace a crushed artery in your stomach that pumps blood into your left leg. We think we got it hooked up in time."

"In time?" I asked. "In time for what?"

He went on to explain that the human body can only withstand the absence of blood flow for approximately six hours. Any more than that and gangrene sets in.

He then proceeded to pull back the covers on my left leg. My calf was seriously swollen! It had literally swelled to the size of a watermelon and reminded me of one of Popeye's arms. It had two eight-inch incisions that formed two wedges, one on each side of my calf. The surgeon informed me that this was done to alleviate the enormous pressure of the swelling.

He added, "We think we repaired the artery in time and that you will be able to keep your leg. We'll have to wait and see."

I was stunned and had a hard time taking it all in.

After the surgeon had left the room, I asked my mom about my friends in the car. She slowly moved closer to my bed and I could tell something was troubling her. "Danny," she said, "Henry is doing well. He just had surgery to repair his broken right leg. His femur was shattered in a number of spots, and they had to insert some pins and rods, but he will be alright. He also lost some of his front teeth, but a dentist will be able to fix that. Jessica is home. She broke her arm and sustained a concussion. Most likely, she will make it to the first day of school in a week."

"Mom," I asked nervously, "how is Sarah?"

"Danny..." she paused. "Sarah didn't make it. She died at the scene of the accident."

I lay speechless, in a state of shock as my room filled with activity once again. I couldn't believe it. Somehow, a part of me knew, but the other part of me refused to accept it. In my semi-sedated state, it was all too much to take in.

I lived in a state of denial for many days. I denied the doctor's report regarding my condition, and I would not accept the fact that Sarah was gone. It was the only way I could cope and get from one moment to the next.

Crazy Contemplation:

It is crazy how quickly our lives can become "absurdly out of place." One day everything can be going well; then, without notice, everything changes.

If you have ever built a house of cards, you know how fragile the structure is. No matter how high, strong or impressive it may look, all it takes is a little bump or an untimely sneeze and the house will fall into a heap leaving no card standing. On August 29, 1986, my life resembled the collapse of a house of cards. All my earthly hopes, along with my identity, were destroyed in a moment.

I've learned that if our greatest hope is not eternally secure, it will eventually topple like that house of cards and not far behind will be the collapse of our identity.

The notion that we are in control of our circumstances and their outcomes is a farce. Change inevitably happens, and we will be left to deal with our limitations time and again, which can produce enormous frustration, worry, and anxiety.

Those who spend great time and effort trying to prevent change only find themselves changed for the worse. They become defensive, overbearing, greedy, hoarders, self-protective, isolated, and lonely. So, is there anything we can do?

Jesus dealt with the issue of change with His disciples on the night of His betrayal. They were about to experience the collapse of their house of cards. For three years, believing Jesus to be the long-awaited Messiah, the disciples had given up everything and invested all they had in Him. However, on the final night, He told them it was all about to change.

Jesus attempted to prepare His disciples by headlining the events that would unfold over the following days; but the disciples weren't ready. Scripture says that "sorrow filled their hearts" (John 16:6). The news of Jesus' coming betrayal, torture and death proved too much for them, eclipsing the glorious promise of His triumphant resurrection on the third day.

It was on this night that Jesus gave the answer for how to live in a world of trouble and continuous change: *"Do not let your heart be troubled; believe in God, believe also in Me"* (John 14:1).

In essence, Jesus says, "Even when everything in life seems to be falling apart—when you observe all your hopes dashed against the rocks, and your preconceived notions and expectations fail—believe (trust) in God. Even when everyone betrays and abandons you, and when darkness and evil seem to prevail and life looks like it's coming to an end, believe (trust) in Me." But how?

In chapters 14-16, Jesus proceeds to give His disciples (and us) the understanding, tools, and reasons why they can trust Him. He ends His discourse with a solemn declaration and promise:

"I have told you these things, so that in Me you may have peace. In this world you will have trouble [tribulations, changes, pressures, suffering, heartaches, disappointments, tragedy, etc.]. But take heart! I have overcome the world."
(John 16:33)

Although the disciples failed to trust Jesus over the next couple days—devastated as they were by His arrest and crucifixion—on the third day, after experiencing the resurrected Christ... EVERYTHING FOREVER CHANGED!

CHAPTER 5

appearing absurdly out of place:

A Crazy Turn of Events—from Casual to Chaos

Part II

The following ten days were some of the longest days of my life. They were like being on a roller coaster with twists and turns, ups and downs. One day, a doctor would give an optimistic report informing me it was likely that I would keep my leg. The next day, a doctor would come in saying I would likely lose it.

Sensing the enormous pressure of the doctor's reports, I frantically tried to move my leg and toes. I knew I only had a few days to prove I was fine, and if I couldn't, bad things would happen.

But nothing moved. At times, I fooled myself into thinking I had moved a couple toes. I even tried convincing the nurses who daily re-bandaged the gaping wedges on my swollen calf. They would always leave me with a reassuring word, "Even though there is no movement, the wound still looks good!"

In my heart, I knew something was terribly wrong. Immobilization was only part of the problem. In addition, there was a burning ache climbing up my leg, and no one could give me a solid answer for the increasing pain. The overarching hope and assumption was that my circulation might be reviving and healing was in process.

After ten days in the hospital, I was scheduled for an exploratory surgery on my leg, and I was more than ready. The pain was now excruciating and I needed relief.

After the surgery, I slowly awoke from the anesthesia and noticed that not only had the pain subsided, but I could feel my leg again! Hearing voices in the room, I opened my eyes to find a team of doctors and my parents standing around my bed. With heartfelt thankfulness, I smiled and said, "Thank you for saving my leg!"

The surgeon's response will be forever etched in my mind: "I'm sorry, Danny. We could not save your leg.

Underneath the pink flesh we discovered gray tissue. Unfortunately, gangrene had been climbing up your leg this entire time."

"What?! But I can feel my leg!" I argued.

"Danny," my mom interjected, "you need to look under the covers."

I swallowed hard, took a deep breath, and raised my bed to an inclined position. As I slowly lifted up the sheets, I was shocked! I just stared at the remaining portion of my leg. It was nothing more than a stump!

"Danny," the surgeon explained, "the gangrene had spread further than we suspected. Unfortunately, we needed to amputate three-and-a-half inches above the knee." I just sat there in disbelief. My worst fear had become my new reality.

Not wanting to upset my parents any more than they already were, I slowly lowered the covers. With stoic dismay, I said, "I can live with this."

Although I appeared calm on the outside, on the inside a fierce storm was raging. Sarah was gone; my leg was gone; and my hope of playing baseball was gone! Was there anything else left to lose?

After the amputation, my kidneys shut down, so I started the process to begin dialysis once a day. Incisions were made in both my wrists, but each procedure failed. A physician finally decided to shove a stint down through the upper part of my chest.

Awake during the procedure, I could hear the crunching and felt the pressure of the stint tearing through my chest muscle. It was a very painful experience. Fortunately, this final procedure was successful, and my dialysis was ready to begin.

Up to this point, all I had been given were ice chips to suck on from time to time. After a number of days, I would have given anything for a drink of water. The A&W Root Beer television commercials were not helping either. They were driving me mad!

After a couple days of dialysis, a different nurse, one whom I had not seen before, asked me if I wanted something to drink during dialysis. "Ah, I wish! But I'm not allowed to drink anything," I explained to her.

She replied, "That's true, you're not allowed to drink anything when you're off dialysis, but when you are on dialysis you can drink whatever you want." Those were some of the most glorious words I had heard in days!

Still not fully convinced, I asked, "Could I have a six-pack of A&W Root Beer?"

"Sure!" she said angelically. "I will order it up for you."

It didn't take long for my order to arrive, and within minutes I had guzzled down the whole six-pack. A few seconds after the last can was emptied, the whole six-pack came spewing back out of my mouth! It was like opening up a new two-liter bottle of Coke right after it has fallen to the ground. But it was worth it! It was the best root beer I had ever had!

As the dialysis started working and my excruciating leg pain diminished, I started to feel better. As a result, the doctors encouraged me to start stretching. I was instructed to begin putting on and taking off my right shoe.

However, as I leaned over for the first time, I felt a searing pain in my lower back. A CAT scan was ordered and the results revealed a crushed disc in my lower back. I was quickly prepared for another surgery.

The damage to my back was extensive. The surgeons removed the natural forty-five degree curvature in my spine and fused it together using two seven-inch Harrington Rods. I now had what is called a "flat back." I would experience major issues from this initial surgery years later.

After surgery, the pain returned with a vengeance, and as the anesthesia wore off, I became hysterical. The nurses tried settling me down, but it was no use. The pain and emotional loss were too much to bear, and I couldn't take it anymore. The nurse tried giving me a shot of Demerol, but I freaked out. "NO!" I yelled. "I can't take any more pain!"

It took my mom and two other nurses to hold me down while a third nurse administered the shot. I was so tense that when she inserted the needle into my flexed upper arm, it bent. Somehow, she managed to inject the narcotic into my system, and within a few minutes I drifted off to sleep.

Before being released from the hospital, I received a hard plastic, custom-made back brace. I was instructed to wear it religiously for half a year.

A couple days after my spinal surgery, a doctor entered my room and shut the door behind him. He had a somber look on his face. Clutching his clipboard in both hands, he slowly walked over to the foot of my bed and stated, "Danny, I have some bad news. I am afraid that because of the injuries you received, you will not be able to have children of your own. I'm sorry."

As a fifteen-year-old, this bit of news did not hit me until later on. In the moment, it was just another thing to be added to the overall package of disappointment—the final nail in my proverbial coffin.

After four weeks in the ICU, I was sent to Providence Hospital to start physical therapy and rehabilitation. It was a long and painful process.

During the first week, I was cast for my first prosthesis. The gentlemen from Cornerstone Prosthetics had also made my back brace. They were always upbeat, humorous, and kind. A news report revealed that they had successfully created an artificial limb for a three-legged horse. These men were crucial in helping me gain some encouragement and courage during a very low time in my life.

I still remember the first time I stood up using an artificial limb. Before the accident, my height was five-foot ten. Now, with a straightened spine, I stood with a six-foot frame. Not bad for laying in bed for five weeks!

I was weak and frail and terrified to take my first step. I held onto the steel parallel bars with a death grip. Taking a step was a great challenge; walking to the other end seemed impossible.

For the first time in my life, I felt fragile. Like a brittle china vase that, if dropped, would shatter into a thousand pieces. Just five weeks earlier, I was taking hits from senior varsity football players; now I would have been afraid to play with toddlers. I knew it was going to be a process physically, but I wasn't prepared for the mental agony that loss generates.

Rehabilitation lasted four weeks. Every day was painful, every day exhausting. It made the memory of football practice seem like a walk in the park. The physicians had said on a number of occasions that if I had not been in excellent physical shape at the time of the accident, I would never have survived. Indeed, I had survived, but what in the world for? As far as I was concerned, there was nothing left.

Crazy Contemplation:

After those eight weeks in the hospital, my whole life was completely crazy, "appearing absurdly out of place." My life before the accident felt like a dream, and I was now trapped in a nightmare that consisted of physical pain and emotional loss. It was like someone had picked up the pages of my life and sent them through a shredding machine. I was being forced to start over, and I didn't like the beginning chapter.

Maybe you've been forced to start over when life as you knew it suddenly changed. Although the transition can be extremely frightening, it's not the end. In fact, it can be the beginning of something wonderful.

When the masks we wear are torn from our faces and we're no longer able to pretend we are something we are not, we have the great opportunity to discover who we really are!

On the night Jesus was betrayed, His whole life changed. His earthly ministry ended; His friends deserted Him; His enemies were given the upper hand; and evil was allowed to prevail. However, there was one thing that did not change for Jesus: His greatest hope and true identity.

Because Jesus knew who He was, to whom He belonged, and why He was here, it gave Him the security and power to love the unlovable and serve the undeserving.

*Jesus, knowing that the Father had given all
things into His hands, and that He had come
forth from God and was going back to God, got
up from supper, and laid aside His garments;
and taking a towel, He girded Himself. Then He
poured water into the basin, and began to wash
the disciples' feet and to wipe them with the
towel with which He was girded. (John 13:3–5)*

Jesus' life and actions reveal what we are capable of when we know our true identity.

Jesus' true identity was affirmed at the beginning of His earthly ministry. After He came up from the water at His baptism, a voice from heaven declared, *"This is my beloved Son in whom I am well pleased"* (Mark 1:11).

However, just like us he does to us, the evil one immediately went after the one thing that could derail Jesus' entire life, mission, and ministry. Satan attacked His identity.

After His baptism, Jesus was immediately led into the wilderness for forty days and nights. Three major temptations came during His time of greatest weakness, and all three were tied together with the same underlying question: Who are you really? They were designed to undermine Jesus' true identity, and Jesus would have to choose whose voice He would listen to and heed.

The following is taken from Matthew 4:1-8:

The first temptation: "If you are the Son of God, turn these stones to bread." Do you hear it? "If you are, then *do*." Or, "Do in order to be." Fortunately, Jesus had already made up His mind to heed "*every word that proceeds out of the mouth of God.*" He knew His "being" did not come from "doing."

The second temptation: "If you are the Son of God, throw yourself down (from the pinnacle of the Temple)..." Do you hear it? "If you are, then prove it!" Or, "Prove yourself in order to be." Again, Jesus knew His true identity was already established. He did not have to prove anything to anyone, including Himself. He fully trusted what the Father had already pronounced, "You are my beloved Son in whom I am well pleased."

If Jesus had succumbed to this temptation, He would have put God to the test, showing disbelief in the validity of His Father's word. Instead, He chose to believe what God had already declared to be true.

The third temptation: "Again, the devil took Him to a very high mountain and showed Him all the kingdoms of the world and their glory; and he said to Him, 'All these things I will give you, if you fall down and worship me.'" Do you hear it? "If you deny your true identity and worship me, I will grant your heart's desire." Or, "Acquire in order to be."

I believe this third temptation was the most tempting for Jesus. In essence, the devil was offering Jesus a counterfeit identity and reality. "If you are willing to sacrifice your allegiance to God, I will give you everything without the pain, the suffering, the humiliation and death your Father has prepared for you. If you worship me, I will give you everything now!"

Thankfully, Jesus never wavered. Again, He knew who He was, to whom He belonged, why He had come, and where He was going. Knowing this gave Him the security, contentment, and power He needed to endure the most heinous torture and death to become the Savior of the world who now sits at the right hand of the Father.

These three temptations continue to allure many today to the counterfeit reality where identity is formed through doing, proving, or acquiring. However, Jesus came to show us what is true and to reconcile us back to God. If we instead choose to trust God's word and His promises, we will receive the same affirmation that was given to Jesus at His baptism: "You are my beloved son, in you I am well pleased."

"Glory to God in highest heaven, and peace on earth to those with whom God is well pleased." (Luke 2:14)

With whom is God well pleased? Only with those who receive His Son.

But as many as received Him, to them He gave the right to become children of God, even to those who believe in His name. (John 1:12)

Those who heed God's voice above all other voices find their true eternal identity as a child of God. He has already declared who we are. It's up to us to believe and receive Him.

It seems relatively easy to believe we are being blessed by God when everything is going well. The challenge is to believe we are equally as blessed in times of tribulation and trial—perhaps even more so. When we experience times of struggle, depression, anxiety, pain, and conflict, we are more likely to look towards the only One who is able to help.

> *"I will lift up my eyes to the mountains; from where shall my help come? My help comes from the Lord, Who made heaven and earth."*
> *(Psalm 121:1–2)*

Even if everything else changes, the most important thing never does. Our true eternal identity will always give us the security, contentment and power to persevere through anything. It is the key that unlocks the true meaning and purpose of life.

But in my state of extreme loss, I was determined to find another hope and identity apart from God.

Chapter 6

intensely anxious or eager; impatient:
Drastic Changes Make Me Crazy

The four seasons—winter, spring, summer and fall—serve many great purposes, especially spring and fall. These two seasons act as gradual transition periods that help us prepare for and adapt to the extreme temperatures of winter and summer.

Entering winter without the buffer of fall would create a climate shock of immense proportions. Winter's icy air would bite all the harder, and the golden glow of summer would be swallowed up by the harsh grey of winter. It would be like boarding a plane in the heat of Death Valley, Arizona, and stepping out into the frozen climate of Vostok, Antarctica. Each season possesses different rhythms and activities, and each provides ample time for transition into the next.

After eight weeks in the hospital, it was time for me to go home. I had been admitted at the tail end of summer and was released in November into the beginning stages of winter.

The few months following my discharge were one of the hardest transition periods of my life. I was thoroughly unprepared to accept all the changes and limitations that disability forces upon a person. It seemed as if everything had either changed or died. My summer had turned to winter, and I'd had no fall season to adapt to the barrenness, no gradual time of transition to adjust to the cold. Summer was gone, winter had come, and I'd had no time to prepare.

The house itself had changed. In order to bring me home, my parents had needed to make the house wheelchair accessible (ADA approved). The side door now had a wheelchair ramp. The furniture was rearranged to accommodate my chair, and my entire bedroom had been moved from the attic to the main floor.

My family had also changed. It was obvious that my accident and Sarah's death had deeply impacted them, some for the better and some for the worse.

My older brother Brian, for instance, clung to his newfound faith in Jesus Christ. I could tell he was different. My "little brother status" had changed in his mind from me being a source of irritation to someone needing salvation. In other words, he actually started to care and have compassion for me. He was sorry for ignoring me and tried often to make amends, so much so that his "big brother status" changed in my mind from him being *someone with salvation* to *a source of irritation.*

When my birthday rolled around at the beginning of January, Brian actually took the time to pick out a birthday card for me. I will never forget it. His intentions were good. With a new heart filled with God's love, genuine concern, and holy zeal, he saw his opportunity to save his little heathen brother who had nearly met his Maker just weeks prior. From what I remember, the card said something like, "Happy Birthday Danny... I love you, but you are going to hell." My pagan friends and I had a heyday with that card in the months and years that followed.

My little sister Cheri, on the other hand, only grew in her feisty attitude. Not realizing the depth of my emotional pain, she decided to entertain herself one day by stealing my artificial limb and wheelchair. I was in no teasing mood. "Cheri, bring them back!" But she was not finished with her little rouse, and I became angry, "Cheri, bring back my leg and wheelchair!!" No answer. Then I did something I had never done before. I panicked! In desperation, I screamed, "Cheri, I need my leg and wheelchair!!!"

Unaware of my fragile state, she had no intention of returning my items anytime soon. This was another breaking point for me. All the loss, pain, and permanent change had left me extremely vulnerable, frail, and terrified. In that moment everything hit me like a ton of bricks. I pushed my face into my pillow and began to scream and sob with hopeless abandon. I was broken, and nothing was ever going to be the same. I wept uncontrollably for nearly an hour.

My mom finally intervened and made my sister return my things. I don't think Cheri ever did say she was sorry, but she never took my leg and wheelchair again.

My parents had changed too. I had sensed them drifting apart for quite some time, but my accident seemed to speed up the process. My mom developed another life outside our family and spent most evenings playing bingo with her friends. Being the passive father that he was, my dad said very little. Something was festering inside him that I would not learn about until years later; for now, all he could do was hang on to his hope of one day retiring from his job.

I had changed as well. I didn't care anymore. Without realizing it, I began to grow cold and callous. Fear became something that I dealt with on a daily basis—fear of the unknown, fear of the future, fear of losing the people closest to me, fear of going back to school, fear of living with a permanent disability, and ultimately, a newfound fear of death.

My confidence was gone. I had been stripped of everything, and I felt naked, alone, and fully exposed. I needed a glimpse of hope, but it would not come in the wintertime.

It was hard for me to accept that Sarah was gone. Her funeral had been held while I was in the hospital, and I didn't even know where she was buried. With no sense of closure, my mind began to play tricks on me.

Now that I was home, the silence was deafening. Sarah and I had spent many hours talking on the phone over the summer. Now, every time the phone rang, my first thought was, "It's Sarah!"

I've experienced that our minds will go to great lengths to generate ways of coping with tragedy and loss. One of those times happened shortly after I returned home.

As I sat in my bedroom, alone with my thoughts, my eyes scanned the room and landed on a half-filled helium balloon that had been brought home from the hospital. As I read the phrase "Get Well Soon," the foil balloon started to move.

Suddenly, I sensed something in the room. "Sarah?" I thought to myself.

Then I did something I had never done before and have never repeated. I had a conversation with the balloon. "Sarah, is that you? Sarah, I miss you."

To my amazement, the balloon began to descend as though it were communicating back. "Sarah, if it is you, let me know you're here and bring me the balloon."

My eyes widened as the balloon began to slowly drift towards me. Thoughts of Sarah flooded my mind and a cold shiver ran up my spine. I started to believe she was in the room.

As the balloon drifted closer to my bed, my heart leapt with joy. I began to feel something I hadn't felt for months: hope! Overwhelmed with emotion, my eyes began to fill with tears.

The balloon drifted around the foot of the bed and down the side I was facing. It continued until it was level with my face and hovered there just beyond my grasp, seeming to stare at me.

I spoke to the balloon, "Sarah, I know it's you! I miss you!"

I believed that if I could just hold the string in my hand, it would be like holding Sarah one last time. I stretched as far as I could, but it was beyond my reach.

For nearly five minutes, the balloon just hovered there taunting me. Then, all of a sudden, it began to ascend and floated back to where it had started. As I watched it float away, great sorrow and disappointment filled my heart.

This incident would serve as a prophetic and graphic picture of the next few years of my life—of the fleeting moments that hope floated ever so close, causing me to believe, only to elude my grasp.

Such is wintertime, when all desires and expectations are taken away, and we wonder if it is worth the effort to ever hope in anything again.

Crazy Contemplation:

There's a condition that can drive us crazy, making us "intensely anxious or eager and impatient": change.

Many years ago, I had the privilege of caring for an elderly gentleman named Dave. Dave was an accomplished businessman who had owned a successful grocery store in Granite Falls for over two decades. He and his wife had wonderful plans to travel around the world after he retired and sold the store.

Dave found his identity in doing and placed his greatest hope in what he would one day acquire. However, drastic changes re-directed Dave's life. A month after he retired, his wife died suddenly. Two months later, as he was still mourning her loss, Dave's lungs began to fail. The lack of oxygen wreaked havoc on his body.

When I arrived on the scene, Dave was bedridden with severe COPD. He had developed a wound on his leg that would not heal and was receiving oxygen treatment. Dave, who had always been upbeat and ahead of the game, was now sullen and defeated.

By God's divine providence, I arrived on the final day the nurse would be giving Dave in-home care. As a result, the baton was passed off to me. The nurse showed me how to undress and bandage his wound, and for the next several months, I stopped in to dress Dave's wound every other day. We had many conversations about God and hope.

Near the end of his life, Dave made a confession I will never forget. "Dan," he said, "all my life I believed that I was always in control. But now, I realize I have never been in control."

It took Dave nearly seventy years to admit this stark, yet truthful, reality. Now, totally dependent on others for his very survival, Dave was humbled and broken.

Although Dave was finally at a place where he was willing to have a conversation about God, he refused to place his trust in Him. For most of his life, Dave had held onto a deep resentment towards the Giver and Taker of life, ever since his daughter had died suddenly of a brain aneurysm on her sixteenth birthday. I can sympathize with Dave because when Sarah died, it felt like she had been taken from me. It caused deep anger and pain.

But sooner or later, we all need to make a choice. We can choose to remain bitter and focus our attention on all that we never got to experience, or we can choose to be thankful for the time we *did* spend with the loved one and the memories we gained. Bitterness leads to hopelessness; thankfulness leads to hopefulness.

In addition, true hope fills in the missing piece of the equation. It recognizes that death is not the end; it's only the beginning. When our perspective is limited to the few years of existence we have on planet earth, it's nearly impossible to get over loss; however, when our perspective encompasses eternity, the unbearable becomes bearable.

Our life on this corrupted earth is short compared to the bliss of eternity. It's like choosing to joyfully endure the few hours of hassle at the airport because you know you're about to board a flight to enjoy a four-week, all-expenses paid vacation at a luxury resort in the Bahamas. Perspective is everything.

Unfortunately, Dave had allowed the root of his bitterness to grow too deep, and it prevented him from receiving God's offer of eternal hope in Christ. I begged Dave to place his hope in Christ and to receive His love, grace, and forgiveness; but in the end, Dave refused to receive the one thing he needed most.

In essence, he couldn't do it. After years of rejecting the guaranteed hope of salvation offered daily by the Savior, Dave went to his grave holding onto his crazy false hope. He died believing the lie that God cannot be trusted.

He would not believe

The Savior's Suffering;

He would not receive

The Savior's Offering;

He would not concede

The Savior's Sovereignty;

He could not believe,

The Savior's Presence flee;

He will now receive

A Savior-less eternity.

Come now, you who say, "Today or tomorrow we will go to such and such a city, and spend a year there and engage in business and make a profit." Yet you do not know what your life will be like tomorrow. You are just a vapor that appears for a little while and then vanishes away. Instead, you ought to say, 'If the Lord wills, we will live and also do this or that.' But as it is, you boast in your arrogance; all such boasting is evil. Therefore, to one who knows the right thing to do and does not do it, to him it is sin. (James 4:13–17)

CHAPTER 7

extremely annoyed or angry:
Limitations Drive Me Crazy!

On New Year's Eve, I said goodbye to 1986. Since everything had changed, I didn't really know what to think and neither did my friends. So, I discovered something that seemed to help the pain go away. I started drinking alcohol, and I drank… and drank… and drank.

After the new year, it was time to enter back into my sophomore year of high school. I still vividly remember my first day back.

My classmates had heard a rumor that I was returning, so many of them greeted me at the front entrance. I can only imagine what they must have thought as I rolled up in my wheelchair with an enormous back brace, an artificial limb strapped around my waist, and a colostomy bag intact and tucked away. It was weird.

Some of my classmates seemed overly friendly, while others remained distant. I could tell this was hard for everyone. Thankfully, Henry was there. He had already been attending school for a number of months, but he was still on crutches.

I felt bad when he told me more about his injuries. Come to find out, it was his shattered leg I was propping myself up on while we were trapped in the car. No wonder he'd wanted me off his leg!

Jessica, who had been sitting in the passenger seat in front of me, was doing well. But even though she had suffered the least amount of physical injuries, she never seemed quite the same.

When I heard details about Sarah, it left me speechless. I couldn't imagine the horror she must have experienced in the final moments of her life. A seasoned fireman named Jeremy, who was on the scene, gave me his eyewitness testimony: "Danny, it was the worst accident I had ever attended. Not only was the ground slick, but it was also covered with sockets from a tool chest that was ejected from the green Gremlin automobile that hit the Honda Civic you were riding in. The man who hit you must have been a mechanic heading home from work. The sockets acted like ball bearings as the firemen rushed around to extract you all from the mangled wreckage.

"Sarah was the last one to be extracted because she was being crushed by the motor. It was literally sitting on her lap. It took a series of maneuvers to cut away at the car in order to get her unpinned. She was conscious and able to communicate with us. The enormous pressure of the engine was preventing her from bleeding out. Unfortunately, once everything was in position, we reached the point where we needed to extract her from the automobile."

Then Jeremy looked me soberly in the eyes, "Danny, when we backed off the motor, Sarah let out a loud scream, and she was gone. I can still remember her scream. It was awful!"

Almost three decades later, Jeremy still retains vivid memories of that horrible scene that continue to haunt his thoughts from time to time.

[Side note: I can't describe the deep appreciation I have for all of you first responders who witness such

tragedies. You are truly our modern-day heroes! I would not be alive today without your bravery and the sacrifice you make on a daily basis! At a chaplain's training conference, I was informed that most of the time, you are able to forget the tragedies you have seen; however, there are always one or two that you can never erase from your mind no matter how hard you try. You have seen and heard things that have altered you, plaguing your memories, and you live with them in the silence of your soul. You have sacrificed a great deal, and you have my utmost honor and respect.]

For the longest time, I lived in a perpetual state of fear that kept me physically immobilized and mentally paralyzed. I took no risks and stayed in my wheelchair for a long time—too long. My friends took note of my apprehension and decided one day that I needed an "intervention."

During this time, I had also become best friends with Anthony. Anthony was a big teddy bear that could morph into a grizzly whenever the situation called for it. He was an excellent bodyguard to have on hand. Even though Anthony didn't have the best upbringing, he was always positive and uplifting. Eventually, he moved in with my family, and we bonded like brothers. Like no one else, Anthony helped me mourn the loss of Sarah and deal with other issues that were holding me back.

One day, when Anthony, Henry, and I were hanging out in my backyard, the "intervention" began. "It's time to start walking, Dan," Anthony strongly suggested.

I quickly countered, "I can't. What if I fall? I'll break something."

Henry, who was still on crutches, suggested I start using the crutches I had received when I left the hospital. "Yeah, I don't know where they are. I'll find them later," I responded.

"I already grabbed them for you," Anthony announced as he walked back from the house. I could see that I was not going to skirt my way out of this. They had made up their minds that it was time for me to stand and take my first steps.

Thanks to their strong persuasion and unwavering confidence, I finally stood up for the first time outside the safety of the parallel bars. My friends helped me take the first few steps into the beginning of a new chapter in my life. Their encouragement was a big part of my healing process, and I began living my life once again in an upright, standing position.

Crazy Contemplation:

Disabilities have two facets that can drive someone crazy, causing them to become "extremely annoyed or angry." One facet is the physical limitation. The second is not so obvious. It is the mental setback.

My friends were so instrumental in my recovery process because they helped me overcome the mental barrier. Although I was now permanently disabled, to them, it was a temporary setback. They believed in me during a time when I was incapable of believing in myself. They always seemed to know when to push and when to be quiet. Without their help I would have focused all my attention on the *"dis-"* and not on the *"-ability."*

Even today, when I read the definition of disability, certain words stand out:

Disability: 1. *lack of* adequate power, strength, or physical or mental ability; *incapacity*. 2. a physical or mental *handicap*, especially one that *prevents* a person from living a full, normal life.[3]

The synonyms are no better: *disqualification, incompetence, incapability, impotence, inability.*[4]

Sometimes, the mental aspect can restrict people even more than the physical. But what if, in God's economy, disability is not a disqualifier? What if disability is actually an advantage?

Interestingly, in a curriculum produced by the University of Washington entitled "Understand Your Abilities and Disabilities," a college student with mobility impairments makes a keen observation: "We should focus on the ABILITY in disability more than the DIS... If we can do that, then we are more apt to succeed."[5] The curriculum also mentions how the effects of disabilities can be minimized by learning to see adversity in a new light.

---

[3] Dictionary.com, s.v. "disability," accessed November 25, 2020, https://www.dictionary.com/browse/disability?s=t.

[4] Ibid.

[5] University of Washington, "Chapter 7. Understand Your Abilities and Disabilities" (University of Washington: Seattle, 1992-2020), https://www.washington.edu/doit/sites/default/files/atoms/files/Chapter-7-Understand-your-abilities-and-disabilities.pdf.

So let's take a moment to see adversity in a new light. In God's eyes, what if our adversities are really advantages? What if disabilities actually give us a greater ability to discover our true identity and purpose in life?

If our true identity can never be found in doing, proving, or acquiring, then having those hopes stripped away may just be the best thing that could happen to us. When false hope is removed, true hope can be obtained.

In other words, when the strengths and talents that often make up our false sense of identity are taken away, we are left with an opportunity to discover that our true identity comes from God alone. Consequently, in light of eternity, an earthly handicap or limitation can prove to be an invaluable gift.

The Apostle Paul certainly seemed to think so. After receiving a handicap—"a thorn" in his flesh—he wrote the following:

> *Because of the extravagance of those revelations, and so I wouldn't get a big head, I was given the gift of a handicap to keep me in constant touch with my limitations. Satan's angel did his best to get me down; what he in*

fact did was push me to my knees. No danger then of walking around high and mighty! At first I didn't think of it as a gift, and begged God to remove it. Three times I did that, and then He told me, "My grace is enough; it's all you need. My strength comes into its own in your weakness." Once I heard that, I was glad to let it happen. I quit focusing on the handicap and began appreciating the gift. It was a case of Christ's strength moving in on my weakness. Now I take limitations in stride, and with good cheer, these limitations that cut me down to size—abuse, accidents, opposition, bad breaks. I just let Christ take over! And so the weaker I get, the stronger I become. (2 Corinthians 12:7–10, MSG)

What is success anyway? Is it the ability to conquer the world like Alexander the Great? Or is it the ability to trust God to the point of death like Jesus Christ? One requires *my* effort, faith in *myself,* and depends on the power of *my* body and mind. The other requires self-denial, faith in God, and depends on the power and wisdom of God.

Alexander's life is an example of how the world defines success; Jesus' life illustrates how God defines success. If it is the latter success we seek, then any kind of disability, ailment, sickness, weakness, handicap, or limitation can become our greatest asset—the quicker we learn to depend on Christ, the greater our success will be in God's eyes.

Jesus clearly taught His disciples this divine principle in John 15:5: *"I am the vine, you are the branches; he who abides in me and I in him, he bears much fruit, for **apart from me you can do nothing**"* (emphasis mine).

The Apostle Paul affirmed, *"I can do all things through him who strengthens me"* (Philippians 4:13).

Unfortunately, in my early life, I was driven by the world's definition of success. It warped my identity and almost destroyed me as it did Alexander the Great. Apparently, Alexander fell sick after a prolonged banquet and drinking bout and died at the age of 32. Maybe he was poisoned, maybe not, but it is interesting to examine the fruit of his labors.

Earnestly believing himself to be a god, Alexander failed to elect a successor. Consequently, within a year of his death, his army and empire broke into a multitude of warring factions, only to be swallowed up by the Roman Empire soon after. So much for the fruit produced by worldly success. He will have an eternity to wish he had chosen to pursue success God's way.

> *"And what do you benefit if you gain the whole world but lose your own soul? ... If anyone is ashamed of Me and My message in these adulterous and sinful days, the Son of Man will be ashamed of that person when He returns in the glory of His Father with the holy angels."* (Mark 8:36, 38)

CHAPTER 8

Slang. with great speed or recklessness:
A Crazy, Out-of-Control Life

As time went on, my strength increased. By April 1987, I no longer had to wear my back brace, and the physician assured me that my fused spine was as strong as it had been before the accident. He encouraged me to start lifting weights and to begin exercising again, so I quickly signed up for weightlifting. My muscles began to develop and my confidence increased.

Always appreciating the finer arts, Henry and I were devoted fans of the WWF (Worldwide Wrestling Federation). This was back in the days of Andre the Giant, Hulk Hogan, Jimmy "Superfly" Snuka, "Rowdy" Roddy Piper, Junkyard Dog, George "The Animal" Steele, and Randy "Macho Man" Savage.

Later that summer, Henry and I had a debate. If a wrestler had the choice to possess either speed or strength, which one would give the greater advantage? Henry believed in speed, and I said strength. Our bickering got us nowhere, so in order to settle the dispute, we decided to wrestle one another. The Two-Legger vs the One-Legger.

After a few beers, we made our way outside into the ring (the front yard). When the imaginary bell rang, Two-Legger rushed out of his corner like a gazelle. He managed to land a couple punches as he maneuvered effortlessly around One-Legger. It appeared that speed had the upper hand, that is, until One-Legger got a hold of Two-Legger. It was like a grizzly mauling a gazelle. Needless to say, speed was winning until strength pinned him. Argument solved. Strength always wins!

As I grew stronger, my days began to take on new rhythms and routines, and I started feeling better about myself. New crazy hopes began surfacing that summer.

For starters, I was given one hundred thousand dollars from the insurance company as compensation for the accident and medical expenses. After I got my driver's license, my parents allowed me to use a portion of the money to purchase a 67' Firebird and a 1980 Jeep CJ5.

I enjoyed these for a few months, until the day Henry showed me his dad's 1978 Silver Anniversary Limited Edition black and silver Corvette. It was the sports car chosen to be the official pace car leading the Indianapolis 500 in 1978. I fell in love with it.

It wasn't too hard to convince my parents to let me buy the Corvette. Although they were more than a little reluctant at first, I finally convinced them that a Corvette could really contribute to my healing process.

Henry's dad graciously traded the Corvette for my Firebird and Jeep, plus a few thousand dollars cash. Placing a Corvette in the hands of a young teenage boy was probably not the wisest decision; however, it did help me take my mind off some things, and it definitely turned some heads.

Another crazy hope fell into my lap when my dad found a lawyer who had learned about my accident. Apparently, in 1986, automakers were required to have shoulder harnesses installed in the backseat. The lawyer knew of a few situations like mine. One such incident involved a young teenage boy who had settled for seven million dollars in a lawsuit because the lap belt he was wearing had paralyzed him from the waist down. The lawyer was convinced that three million was almost guaranteed given the extent of my loss and injuries.

This was the greatest news I could have possibly received at that time. My desires and expectations soared through the roof! My crazy hope of acquiring millions led me to entrust my future to wealth, and if I no longer possessed the ability to make millions playing baseball, I now had the means through a lawsuit.

Unfortunately, the knowledge of being financially set for life gave me license to slack off. I replaced studying with cheating. If I would have put more effort into cheating, I am sure I could have graduated with more than a 3.2 grade point average.

By the time I graduated high school, I had never even read a book. My reasoning was simple: "Why stress about studying when I won't have to work anyway? Three million properly invested will allow me to live comfortably."

In my mind, life was beginning to go down a different track. If baseball was no longer an option, the next best thing was to become a Hollywood movie actor. I imagined one day becoming the next James Bond or Nathan Hunt. I wanted to become the first spy actor with the ability to hide concealed weapons in my artificial leg. With that goal in mind, Anthony and I started to make plans to head down to Hollywood, California, after we graduated.

At the time, Granite Falls High School did not have a drama program, so I encouraged the counselors and staff to begin the process of starting one. These crazy hopes gave me the ability to dream again.

I was determined to live stress-free, carefree, and reckless. Drinking became my favorite pastime. If there wasn't a party happening, Anthony, Henry and I created one; and even though we were underage, we mastered the art of acquiring alcohol. We knew who to ask, when to ask, and where to ask. When there was no one available to help us out, we used our fake IDs or we stole it. It was bad.

By age seventeen, I had officially become an alcoholic, and drinking and driving became the norm. At the time, I would have told you that I was simply trying to have a good time. In reality, I was running scared. Filling my time with pleasure was the only way I knew how to escape the disappointments of life.

One night, I was challenged to a race. The person challenging me owned a '68 SS Camaro that was souped up and supercharged. He supposedly had the fastest cars in Snohomish County. We decided to race up at a place called Sand Hill on the Mountain Loop Highway. It had a long straight stretch perfect for burying the speedometer and gave enough room to slow down before the next turn in the road.

We climbed Sand Hill and took our positions. At the signal, we pushed the gas pedals to the floor. Three-quarters of the way down the hill, I looked over at the Camaro next to me. We were at 120 miles an hour and still gaining speed. By the time we reached the bottom of the hill, my speedometer was buried at 140, and I started to pull away from the Camaro for the win.

However, before I could slow down, I hit a swell in the road and for a split second I was airborne. When I connected with the pavement again, the front spoiler was literally ripped off from the impact. To this day, I have no idea where my spoiler went.

For spring break of my junior year, Anthony's dad gave us over a thousand dollars to take a trip from Granite Falls, Washington, to Anaheim, California. We purchased tint for the windows, installed a fake cellular car phone to impress onlookers and a radar detector to warn us of impending police officers. We were determined to make it a non-stop drive.

That was a road trip I will never forget. We took turns, one driving at breakneck speed while the other consumed a six-pack. Once the effects of the alcohol had worn off, we switched. It normally takes a person twenty-one hours to get to Los Angeles, but we made it in eighteen. We learned the art of driving in the fast lane, flashing our headlights to inform people to get out of our way.

As we headed over the mountainous terrain leading into L.A., something was off. Every time I started to doze off, I was startled awake by the sound of screeching tires as we rounded corners. For some reason, Anthony's driving was growing more reckless. Come early dawn, I switched spots with Anthony, and he quickly fell asleep.

An hour later, we were welcomed by the infamous L.A. traffic. Everything around us came to a sudden stop; however, the Vette didn't want to stop. I pushed the brake pedal to the floor, locking up the front left brake.

We slid to a screeching halt and stopped just inches away from the car in front of us.

We pulled off at the next exit and discovered a sobering reality: the master brake cylinder was blown, which meant we had been driving with almost no brakes for hundreds of miles. If the left disc brake had not seized up, we would have suffered a major collision.

Thankfully, Anthony was able to make the repair and we were on our way. We toured Hollywood and every bar and nightclub that accepted our IDs. Towards the end of the trip, we somehow managed to get thrown out of Disneyland for being drunk and disorderly on the Haunted House ride.

We returned home the same way we had driven down but this time with working brakes. It was a trip we will never forget.

I continued in a reckless downward spiral and found myself drawn to the occult. After moving my bedroom back to the attic, Anthony, Henry and I purchased a Ouija board and began having conversations with the dead.

We had no idea what we were doing or what we were opening ourselves up to, but we were drawn in by a mysterious and alluring power. We thought the Ouija board might be able to give us some answers, and I hoped to be able to talk to Sarah again.

Things got even weirder when my friends and I noticed my license plate number. It read: LCY 101. It was obvious to us that LCY stood for Lucy, which was short for Lucifer, and I lived at 101 N. Indiana Ave. I was alright with this conclusion. In my mind, I had already tried God and the "church thing," and from what I could see, religion certainly wasn't helping or providing answers for my dad.

My mind darkened. Horror movies provided me with a steady diet of evil and violence, while heavy metal music helped me foster a bad attitude. Bitterness towards life began to take root in my heart, which led to even more bad choices.

I became lewd and flippant with my words, and my mouth produced nothing but colorful language. In this state of mind, it is not surprising that I found morbid pleasure in blaspheming the name of Jesus Christ over and over again. For some strange reason, it gave me a sense of empowerment. I had a blatant disregard for everything I had been taught about God when I was younger; it disgusted me. I erroneously started to believe that God was deaf, daft, dumb or dead.

There were brief periods of time when Anthony or Henry became interested in God. But whenever Henry started attending church, Anthony and I would harshly tease him out of the idea. Then when Anthony started attending, Henry and I would get on his case. All in all, we did not have one another's best interest in mind.

After months of dabbling in darkness, Anthony and I began noticing strange phenomena. The incidents would happen when either of us was alone in my bedroom. It happened to me once on a night Anthony was gone.

After turning out the lights and getting into bed, I felt the room getting colder and darker. An unnerving chill shot up my spine, and I was overwhelmed by a paralyzing fear that gripped my insides.

As I laid on my right side with my face towards the wall, I heard faint, heavy breathing behind me. At first, I hoped it was my Chinese Pug, but the breathing got louder and closer. It was rhythmic and humanlike. I tried to move, but I couldn't.

The breathing made its way across the room and stopped directly behind my head. Then I felt the breathing on my neck. I wanted to scream! At that moment, whatever had a hold on me finally released its grip, and I quickly rolled over to face the mysterious predator. In an instant, the breathing stopped and I immediately turned on the light to scan the room. I was alone. After that, I made my way downstairs to sleep on the couch with the lights on.

Once Anthony, Henry and I began to share our experiences with one another, we came to a joint consensus: the Ouija board was to be destroyed. The next day, we burned it in the bonfire.

Stories like these characterized my life during those reckless years; yet in the midst of it all, I was being protected and I didn't even know it.

Crazy Contemplation:

We all respond differently after experiencing great loss. My response was crazy, out-of-control and often reckless. The transition period after my accident brought me face to face with my fears and limitations; and since it happened during a time of confusion and rebellion, my responses were radically dysfunctional.

Feeling hopeless, I became fearful. Feeling fearful, I sought to become numb. Feeling numb, I became angry and reckless. Then the cycle would repeat itself. That was how I coped. But ultimately, I was angry with God.

Have you ever been angry with God? It doesn't always lead to drunkenness or a crazy demonic pursuit in the occult; there are countless other ways to act out. However, over many years, I have found the following to be true: whenever we are struggling with bitterness, unforgiveness, or anger towards another person or a situation, the fact is that we are actually angry with God.

Here is my reasoning. If God is truly sovereign, then whatever happens, whether good or bad, God is either the One doing it or He is allowing it.

When I counsel people who are bitter, many resist this idea at first. For the most part, they would rather believe they are doing well in their relationship with God and are simply embittered towards their circumstances or another person. Unfortunately, it doesn't work like that.

Regarding anger towards another person, 1 John 4:20 states, *"If someone says, 'I love God,' and hates his brother, he is a liar; for the one who does not love his brother whom he has seen, cannot love God whom he has not seen."* If this is true, then we are only as close to God as we are to our worst enemy. No wonder Jesus said, *"Love your enemy and pray for those who persecute you"* (Matthew 5:44). Jesus' statement alone can frustrate us because, in and of ourselves, it is impossible to obey! This is precisely the point.

God wants us to come to Him with our anger (as exemplified in many of the Psalms written by David). He has a divine plan that is not meant for our ruin but to bring about total restoration. Next time you find yourself embittered, angry, or unable to forgive, try going to the real source of your anger. Ask God, "Why did You cause or allow this to happen?"

Hopefully, this leads you to ask questions that can begin to bring about healing:

- God, what are You trying to teach me?
- What does my response reveal about my trust in You?
- How do You want me to respond?
- Is there a lie that I am believing?
- What truth do I need to start believing?

The first person to be angry with God was Cain. You can read his story in Genesis 4. In short, Cain was angry because God accepted his brother Abel's offering but rejected Cain's. Genesis 4:6–7 states,

> Then the Lord said to Cain, "Why are you angry? Why is your face downcast? If you do what is right, will you not be accepted? But if you do not do what is right, sin is crouching at your door; it desires to have you, but you must master it."

Unfortunately, Cain's sinful attitude got the best of him, and he murdered his brother. Seen in a different light, Cain killed his brother out of jealous hatred, but ultimately, he was angry with God. Scripture says that our battle is not against flesh and blood; instead, it is a spiritual battle.

It is sobering to know that sin is crouching at our door as well. Its desire is to have us, and no one has ever mastered it! Deep down, just like Cain, we know that our efforts and offerings are insufficient and unacceptable to God. In the book of Romans, God confirms that this is true:

As it is written: 'There is no one righteous, not even one; there is no one who understands, no one who seeks God. All have turned away, they have together become worthless; there is no one who does good, not even one.' (Romans 3:10–12)

... for all have sinned and fall short of the glory of God. (Romans 3:23)

What an inconvenient truth! At times, it gnawed at me; at other times, I blocked it out of my mind. But the truth remained—I was a sinner and I fell short of the glory of God. In other words, I fell short of being everything God had designed and created me to be; I was living in direct, sinful rebellion against Him. This inconvenient truth caused me frustration and anger. For others, this reality can lead them into darkness and hopeless despair.

However, not everyone is hopeless. In fact, there are some who are blessed:

Blessed are those whose lawless deeds have been forgiven, and whose sins have been covered. Blessed is the man whose sin the Lord will not take into account. (Romans 4:7–8)

What greater reality could there be than to know that every lawless deed has been forgiven and no sin is taken into account? Psychiatrist Karl Menninger, who conducted groundbreaking research with the mentally ill, is quoted as saying that 75 percent of psychiatric patients could go home tomorrow if they believed their sins were forgiven!

Forgiveness is the key that unlocks the way of restoration. When our sins are forgiven, we can forgive anyone. When we are perfectly loved, we can love anyone. When we are eternally secure and accepted, we can persevere through anything. We can't give what we have not received.

During this crazy, reckless time in my life, I didn't know forgiveness was an option. As a result, I sank even deeper into the mire and deeper into hopelessness.

CHAPTER 9

unusual; bizarre:

A Crazy Turn of Events—From Chaos to Confusion

In the latter part of my junior year, my family took a vacation to Hawaii. My mom had grown fond of Anthony, so he was allowed to come along. From the parts I remember, Hawaii was absolutely incredible!

One night, Anthony and I saw fit to rip a closet door off its hinges and launch it from the balcony. I think we were going to try and use it as a surfboard. The manager had a long talk with my mom and dad, and they were somehow able to convince the hotel to let us complete our stay.

While Anthony and I got our kicks, my parents were just trying to make it to the end of the vacation. This was the first time I realized that my mom and dad were on their last leg of their marriage. They didn't seem to enjoy one another, and my dad acted like he was being dragged along against his will. They never talked about their troubles, but we definitely witnessed them from a distance.

Upon returning home from Hawaii, Anthony and I had a conversation that would change the course of my life. We asked one another whom we would choose to date at school if given the chance. Anthony chose Tina Gray, and I chose Kim Haverfield. Then Anthony bet me twenty dollars he could date Tina before I could date Kim. We shook hands and Anthony fell asleep.

But I couldn't sleep. All I could think of was, "How will I ever get Kim to like me? We liked each other in middle school, but that was before the accident, before all the changes. I was out of my league then, and I am certainly out of my league now!"

Unbeknownst to me, Kim had become a Christian after she left middle school while attending the youth group at Community Bible Church. For nearly three years, she had dated the pastor's son. Unfortunately, she received a lot of wounds from that septic relationship that left her heart scarred and broken.

Once on fire for God, Kim was now floundering and disillusioned. She backslid in her faith, and I began seeing her more and more at drinking parties. Although she was now on my turf, I didn't have a clue how to proceed. My fear kept me in the dark, just outside the light of the bonfire.

Kim was different and seemed to have it all. She drove a '67 red Ford Mustang that she'd helped her father refurbish. She was the homecoming princess her junior year, first princess her senior year, and voted best all around. She was a cheerleader, popular, athletic, responsible, smart, beautiful, kind, and joyful. She attracted me like a magnet.

Kim's family seemed perfect as well. Her mother was heavily involved in her life, attending and helping out with all of Kim's sporting events and academics. She was a senior class mom and assistant, worked in the lunchroom, and was a big part of the PTA and the Booster Club. Her dad was hardworking and would give a hand and the shirt off his back to anyone.

From all appearances, Kim was raised in the picture-perfect apple pie, two golden labs, fenced yard, meatloaf on Friday Cunningham family. The only difference was in the names. Instead of her redhead brother being Richie, his name was Jimmy Jr.—even better!

All that to say, I was more than a little intimidated. Finally, one moonlit night while standing around a bonfire, I caught her eye. As I moved through the crowd to reach her, I somehow got up the nerve to start a conversation. We talked.

Within a few weeks, we started inquiring whether or not the other was planning on attending an event or party. I started seeking her out during breaks between classes, and I think she did the same. Then we started having lunch together. Slowly and steadily, a good friendship was forming.

Until this point, I hadn't realized just how much Sarah's death had changed me. I was afraid of letting girls get close to me. Not wanting to experience the pain of loss ever again, I became selfish and lived fast and furious in my relationships with the opposite sex. I aimed only to *use* girls in order to avoid the risk love creates; yet my attempts to protect myself only caused others to suffer hurt and loss. This is something I deeply regret.

Kim's senior prom was just a few weeks away, and I had heard through the grapevine that Taylor, my junior high friend and rival, was taking Kim. This was no surprise as they had been dating on and off. I, on the other hand, made plans with a girl I had met in Hawaii. Rosanne was a prom queen in Salem, Oregon, and she was willing to drive five hours up to Washington to go with me.

A week before prom, however, a wonderful thing happened. Rosanne found herself unable to attend. In passing, I mentioned this to Kim who was having second thoughts about going with Taylor. One thing led to another, and the next thing I knew, I was taking Kim Haverfield to her senior prom! Me, a disabled Junior from a dysfunctional family that hardly ever ate apple pie or meatloaf!

Prom night turned out to be one of the most magical and best nights of my life! Kim and I connected on many levels, and our friendship deepened. It became apparent that she saw past my disability and genuinely cared for me as much as I did for her. Our relationship continued throughout the summer of 1988, and, unbeknownst to me, I started to fall in love with her.

As I began my senior year of high school, it was a little strange that my girlfriend had already graduated, but it worked. By this time, I had moved out of my parent's house and was living with a twenty-five-year-old friend named Linus who I had met at a party. My dad could no longer tolerate all the friends I brought over to the house, so I left. This allowed Kim and I to have a lot of privacy.

In October 1988, something happened that would literally change the course of my life. I got Kim pregnant. Needless to say, I was shocked! I wish I could say that I was overjoyed by the fact that the doctors had been wrong in their diagnosis and I could indeed bear children, but I wasn't. All I could think of was how this was going to hurt my plans to pursue an acting career in Hollywood.

In a desperate attempt to prevent my crazy hope from collapsing, I did the most despicable thing imaginable: I tried to coerce Kim into having an abortion. I had a friend who knew someone with access to pills that would produce a miscarriage. Kim was resistant. We argued and fought over it for weeks; but in spite of my attempts, she had made up her mind. She concluded that it was her body, and she was going to have the child.

By Christmas break of my senior year, I was a young man divided and confused. By now, everyone knew Kim was pregnant, except for the few who thought she had duct taped a basketball under her shirt. Since my high school graduation was drawing near, I needed to make a decision regarding my future. Should I leave and live my life in pursuit of my crazy hopes? Or should I stay and be the father to this miracle child I should never have been able to beget? It wasn't an easy decision.

Most of my friends were telling me to leave, including Linus. Linus had already been married and divorced, and we had long talks about the horrors he had experienced while married. Those conversations made me sick to my stomach.

Other friends told me I would be throwing my life away, that Kim would be just fine without me, and that I should pursue my career in acting. I was torn inside and thought, "Why does life have to be so hard? Why do my hopes always seem to elude my grasp?"

In March 1989, Kim (now six months pregnant) flew to Orlando, Florida, for a six-week airline flight attendant academy training she had received as a scholarship. This month and a half gave me a lot of time to think about my life—the past, the present and the future—and the longer Kim was gone, the more I missed her.

I missed her so much, in fact, that I stopped listening to my friends who spoke negatively about marriage and started seeking counsel from those who encouraged me to do the honorable thing, namely, my brother Brian. He not only encouraged me to do the right thing, he also used this time to talk to me about what was most important to him—his faith.

Unbeknownst to me, Brian and his friends had been praying for me and my friends when we were involved in the occult. Deep down, I knew his greatest desire was that I would believe in Jesus. He would say with earnest sincerity, "Dan, all you have to do is believe! You don't have to change at all. Just believe!"

I appreciated his heart, but it was not for me. First off, I had always thought he and his friends were a little weird. But secondly, I knew deep down that what he was saying didn't seem quite right. According to his definition, I was already a Christian. I *did* believe that God and Jesus existed, and I was choosing to live an unchanged life. I figured that if God accepted a person simply on those terms, then God was pretty pathetic.

I'm sure that was not what Brian meant, but that was how I took it. Truth be told, I had never seen anything good come from my dad's faith; after four decades of faithful church attendance, his belief had gotten him nowhere. To me, Christianity seemed impotent.

Kim had been gone for four weeks, and I began wondering if I could really live my life without her and still be happy. She had become the single most important person in my life and my most intimate and closest of friends. I began to realize that I didn't want to live my life without her.

Then it dawned on me that Kim had already won my heart. I really did love her! As soon as I came to this realization, I was all the more anxious for her to return home. I was finally ready to commit myself to her for the rest of my life.

I began planning a special marriage proposal. My brother and I came up with an idea and contacted a popular radio station in the area to work out an agreement. Next, I enlisted Kim's sister to help me find an engagement and wedding ring that Kim would love.

Finally, I arranged to meet with her father in order to get his approval to marry his daughter. Everything was finally set and ready to go, just in time for Kim's return.

On the night of the proposal, I could hardly contain myself. Kim's parents had agreed to make sure she was free of any commitments, appointments or responsibilities. Around 7:45, I stopped by to take her out for a drive. We needed to be parked at the falls, just outside of town, by 8pm. "Mark's Moment of Mush" was broadcasted at 8:10. Everything went according to plan.

As Mark began his moment of mush, I quickly made an excuse to exit the Vette. I walked over to the passenger side, opened Kim's door and knelt down on one knee. "What are you doing?" Kim asked. "I just wanted to be close to you," I replied. "Oh, listen! Mark's Moment of Mush is on." Mark started his commentary, slowly working down his list of radio listeners who had called in earlier to send sweet nothings to a lover. It was like passing a love note to a sweetheart via radio jockey.

At the end of the list, Mark announced a special moment of mush and proceeded to read what I had written up: "To my precious angel, you mean the world to me. I never knew I could love someone the way I love you. You are my best friend, and I feel alive when I am with you. I don't want to live my life without you. Kim, will you marry me? Love, Dan Moushey."

At that exact moment, I opened up a little black velvet box. Kim's eyes lit up as I placed the ring on her finger, while the radio station played the song I had selected. We held hands and embraced as we listened.

I never needed love like I need you.

And I never lived for nobody, but I live for you.

Oooh, babe, lost in love is what I feel when I'm with you.

Maybe it's the way you touch me with the warmth of the sun.

Maybe it's the way you smile, I come all undone.

Oooh, babe, lost in love is what I feel when I'm with you.

Baby, oh I get chills when I'm with you.

Baby, my world stands still when I'm with you;

When I'm with you.

I never cared for nobody like I care for you.

And I never wanted to share the things I want to share with you.

Oooh, babe, lost in love is what I feel when I'm with you.

Baby, oh I get chills when I'm with you.

Baby, my world stands still when I'm with you.

When I'm with you,

When I'm with you,

When I'm with you... [6]

When the song ended, something was still left undone. Kim hadn't given a reply. I thought, "Was the ordeal a bit confusing? Was it too emotional? Or maybe, it was because Mark technically did the asking over the airwaves."

At any rate, I needed an answer. So once again, still on bent knee, I made the proposal as clear as I possibly could, "I never did get your answer. Will you marry me?"

Kim gave the loveliest smile and said, "YES! Of course I will marry you." With that, I gave my co-

---

[6] Sheriff, "When I'm with You," track 4 on *Sheriff*, Capitol Records, 1982, vinyl LP.

conspirators a call and let them know the good news. Mission accomplished!

News about my proposal traveled quickly around the high school, and from that point on, I received nothing but encouragement and support. I was still unsure how Hollywood was going to fit into the future, but for now, I was convinced I had made the right decision. At the very least, I was relieved that we would be financially stable once the lawsuit was finally settled.

By graduation day, it seemed as if the whole town knew Kim and I were engaged. After the graduation ceremony, my classmates and I were carted off to a health club in Arlington that we had rented out for our senior class party. There were chaperones policing our every move, but that did not prevent us from having a good time. I got my hands on a fifth of vodka and started my numbing process. My classmates had agreed ahead of time that we needed to be discrete, lest we lose our opportunity to fly to Disneyland come dawn.

After a few shots of Bacardi 151, I was challenged to a game of racquetball. I knew I was in trouble when I couldn't determine which ball I should hit. In my drunken stupor, I lunged for an imaginary ball and somehow managed to knock myself unconscious.

When I woke up, I was laying on a seat near the back of the bus. As we drove to the airport, my friends filled me in on how they had gotten me through the night and onto the bus undetected. Although they were not very happy, I was extremely thankful.

Disneyland and Knott's Berry Farm were a blast; however, while I was in California, Kim started to have some major contractions back home. Her due date was still a few weeks off, but it appeared she was going to have the baby early. As a result, I caught the next flight home, accompanied by a gigantic stuffed polar bear I had won at Knott's Berry Farm and a giant stuffed Mickey Mouse my classmates had purchased for the baby's arrival.

By the time I got home, the doctor had already diagnosed Kim as having false labor. Although I was a little disappointed, it was good to be home and see Kim doing well.

Kim didn't go into labor until seven days past her due date. When the labor started, we waited at her parents' house for several hours, monitoring her contractions as they grew stronger and closer together.

When we finally decided it was time to go to the hospital, Kim was poised, controlled, and had no sense of urgency; however, she knew I had been looking forward to racing to the hospital when the big day arrived, so she graciously allowed me to fulfill my dream. In my mind, this was the one chance I got to use my trump card excuse: "Officer, my fiancé is in labor!" Sadly, we never got pulled over, and I never got the chance to use it.

At the hospital, Kim gave birth to an 8-pound 2-ounce, 19-inch beautiful baby boy. It was the most incredible thing I had ever experienced! We called him Cody for approximately two hours, but it didn't stick. Finally, we both agreed that he should be named Tanner Ryan Moushey.

Tanner has been a miracle child in so many ways. To this day, he is a daily reminder of how God can bring so much good out of so much bad.

Crazy Contemplation:

Once again, my life took a crazy, sudden turn—this time from chaos to confusion. When I got Kim pregnant, it felt "absurdly out of place." Having children was no longer an option for me—or so I had been told—but God had different plans, and He used it to slow me down.

To be honest, I didn't think I was ready for a serious relationship and certainly not to become a father. However, if not for Kim's pregnancy, I would have missed out on what have become some of my biggest blessings. The protective layers I had placed around myself prevented me from recognizing true love when it appeared. I needed something drastic to snap me out of my selfishness and pride.

Unfortunately, it is easy to make life choices that are selfish and foolish when you don't really know who you are. It still grieves me every time I remember that, if it had been up to me, I would have ended my baby boy's life for the sake of convenience.

It makes me wonder how many other times I have disregarded another person because I was too busy protecting my own crazy hopes. How many times have I neglected the needs of others because I wanted to make sure my crazy hope was fulfilled?

Thanks be to God for His patience and kindness towards us! Even though He knows our every evil thought, sinful act, and rebellious attitude, He still longs to lavish His grace, mercy, love and forgiveness upon us. Even now, He is calling to many, "Come back to Me!"

I can testify with confidence that God is the Master of making all things new. As an eyewitness and one who has personally experienced it, I know for certain that He makes beautiful things out of lives filled with nothing but manure. His kindness really does lead us to repentance (Romans 2:4).

But some people, like my dad, have a longer journey and must pass through more pain before they are ready to accept the peace that God is offering.

CHAPTER 10

mentally insane; demented:
Crazy Suicidal Tendencies

As I was entering into fatherhood and engagement, my dad was entering into isolation and divorce. I wish I had been more aware of his pain and hurt, but I was too focused on situations in my own life.

My dad had placed all his eggs in the "retirement" basket, and he finally received the crazy hope he was after. He couldn't wait to throw off the shackles and responsibility of his position at the DSHS. Retirement was the one thing he had always talked about, believing it would provide the fulfillment and happiness necessary to achieve what had always seemed to elude him: contentment.

I remember attending his retirement party in 1989. Never had I seen my dad happier than he was that day in the company of his coworkers and staff. He was clearly in his element, and he thrived. My eyes were opened as I caught this glimpse behind the curtain to the other side of my dad's life. It was like watching dark storm clouds break apart and the sun burst forth. At his office and with his staff, my dad was giddy, light-hearted, confident and poised.

When his coworkers were given the opportunity to say a few words, no one had anything negative to say. My dad was obviously someone greatly respected and highly valued. Some even requested that he reconsider and postpone his retirement for a few more years.

It was quite obvious that his good leadership was going to be sorely missed by everyone in the building. I was blown away! Not that people liked him, but because his work life stood in stark contrast to everything I had ever witnessed at home.

For as long as I can remember, my dad had played a very passive role in his marriage. Never once did I see him take charge and lead our family. Instead, he used tactics of manipulation and whining whenever he wanted us to do something. For instance, instead of telling us to do the dishes, he would do the dishes himself. Then he would say things under his breath like,

"I don't know why I have to do the dishes. Someone else should be doing these dishes. I had to work all day. No one else had to work all day."

Instead of asking my mom to stay home more often, he would complain when she left, "I don't know why she has to go play that Bingo every night. I don't understand what she sees in that Bingo."

Needless to say, his family didn't have the respect for him that the coworkers at his retirement party had. In fact, a few months prior, my mom had determined that she was finished with their marriage. She had hoped to wait to divorce my dad until after my sister graduated, but she was done wasting her time. When he tried to work it out with her, she told him she was already involved with another man.

Even worse than his wife leaving him, my dad headed into retirement feeling cursed by an awful skeleton in his closet. A priest had once told him that he had committed the unpardonable sin. That is a burden no human being should have to bear. The priest's statement ate at my dad's conscience like cancer, and guilt and shame wreaked havoc in his soul.

With his wife gone and no chance of having his sins pardoned, retirement only served to magnify and exacerbate the devastating disappointment his life had become.

My dad was not prepared to handle the enormity of free time that retirement offered. While sitting in isolation in a dark, empty house, he started on a downward spiral. In six months' time, he had abandoned all health and fitness and become an alcoholic.

Once an avid jogger who ran five miles a day, my dad put on forty pounds within a year. His face became puffy from the consumption of spirits, and his speech slurred as he stammered out lies to cover up his drinking. The television became his only friend and companion. My dad's crazy hope was sinking to the bottom of the abyss, and it was strapped tight to his ankle.

The retirement income he received was insufficient to support his drinking habit, so my dad began collecting everything he could find and selling it in garage sales. Unbeknownst to me, he started searching through my old bedroom as well to find items to sell.

One day, I visited him during one of his sales only to find out he had just sold my Seattle Mariners Alvin Davis batting glove that was given to me while I was in the hospital. I was shocked, not that it was gone, but that he had only sold it for 50 cents!

As I perused what was left of my belongings, I discovered that he had sold most of my treasured items for pennies on the dollar. This included my entire original Star Wars collection, all my action figures, my Imperial Walker, Luke's land speeder, and even the Millennium Falcon. All of it... gone!

I quickly picked through the rest of his sale items and rescued my football signed by the '86 Seahawks. Sarah's father had approached both the Mariners and the Seahawks to tell them about my story right after my leg was amputated. Needless to say, both the football and the batting glove were important to me. As I peeled the 75-cent sticker off the football, I asked, "Dad, don't you realize how much these things mean to me?"

My dad grinned and gave his typical reply, "Ah Danny, it's just junk."

If idle time is the devil's playground, then my dad's mind was like the devil's amusement park. Towards the end of his downward spiral, my dad became suicidal; but thankfully, deep down, he had a greater desire to live.

This was evidenced by the fact that after slitting his wrists, he immediately called 911 and was rushed to the hospital. Another time, he climbed to the roof of our two-story house and threatened to jump off, only to be coaxed down by a Granite Falls fireman.

The final straw came one night when he decided to park his Ford Ranger on some railroad tracks. When the speeding train came around the bend, my dad made a last-minute decision to save himself; however, when he tried driving off the tracks, his tires wedged themselves into the grooves. Realizing that his truck was stuck and impact was seconds away, he dove out the driver's side door and out of the way of the speeding locomotive.

According to my dad's eyewitness account, "When the train smashed into the truck, it was thrown fifty feet from the tracks! It looked like someone had kicked a tin can!"

After a police investigation of the incident, my dad was given mental assistance.

Once my parents' divorce was finalized, my dad moved out of the house and into a small apartment in Everett. Everything he had worked for was gone, and he finally reached a place where he had nowhere to turn.

All of his hopes had been smashed when the bottom of the "retirement" basket fell out.

Thankfully, this is not the end of his story. He may have believed God had given up on him, but nothing could have been further from the truth.

Crazy Contemplation:

Crazy hope that disappoints can lead a person to become "mentally insane and demented." Unfortunately, my dad became a prime candidate when he placed his greatest hope in something attached to this world. Once his hope was gone, his world unraveled.

I don't write these things to shame my dad. On the contrary, I've included this chapter as a warning. Where we place our greatest hope matters because that is ultimately where our identity is formed. This was graphically displayed in my dad's life. His identity was not found in his faith. It was found in his work and in retirement.

Once again, it is so easy to think that our identity stems from what we do, what we can prove, or what we hope to acquire. What a lie! Our true identity comes from the One to whom we belong. In *The Gift of Being Yourself,* author David Benner writes that:

1. True identity is a matter of discovering something that is already there. Identity is not something we create.
2. Our true identity can only be found in the One who gave us our identity.
3. True identity is revealed by God as He reveals Himself to us when we seek to know Him.

> There is no true life apart from relationship with God. Therefore there can be no true self apart from this relationship. The foundation of our identity resides in our life-giving relationship with the Source of life. Any identity that exists apart from this relationship is an illusion.[7]

Crazy hope is always a gamble unless it is placed in the God who created you. He is the One who sustains you, the Savior who redeems you, and the Father who never fails you.

---

[7] David Benner, *The Gift of Being Yourself* (Downers Grove, IL: InterVarsity Press: 2015), 81.

We all place our hope in something or someone. Some have hope that the day of reckoning, or final judgment, will never come. However, before you place your bet, consider the stakes. When placing final bets at the Kentucky Derby, smart gamblers spend hours in careful research and inquiry before they ever arrive at the track. In the race of life, the worst thing that can happen is to discover that you have lost your soul for eternity simply because you didn't take the time to discover the truth about the race itself.

> The race was already run
>
> All the horses lame but one
>
> Ridden by the Owner's Son
>
> Eternal Victory was won!
>
> The Restoration has begun!
>
> The Son now bids us, "Come!"
>
> Before He proclaims, "It's Done!"
>
> (Inspired by Revelation 19:11-16, 21:6-7)

God's ways are entirely different than our ways. We place our bets first and then hope our horse clinches the victory; God first clinches the victory for us and then says, "Place your bets!" If we don't do the research and inquiry, we risk betting our souls on something that has already been determined and sacrificing our eternal existence for something that comes up lame and defeated.

On the Day of Judgment, Jesus will return riding a white horse, not to run the race again, but to receive those who have placed all their HOPE in His sacrifice on the cross at Calvary. God universally announced the victory when He raised His Son triumphantly from the dead. It's not too late to change your bet! Let it all ride on the Risen Savior riding the white horse. The coming King of kings and Lord of lords is near!

Chapter 11

wonderful; excellent; perfect:
CRAZY AWESOME HOPE!

After Tanner was born, I immediately began looking for a place where Kim and I could start living together. I found an apartment about a block away from where I lived, which made the move smooth and easy. However, getting someone to marry us was not so easy.

In mid-July 1989, Kim and I set out to find someone to help us tie the knot. I wanted to get a justice of the peace; Kim, on the other hand, wanted a religious ceremony officiated by a pastor in the area. I was fine with that, respecting her Christian faith and all. So, Kim went to talk to the pastor at Community Bible Church where she had been saved and baptized in the summer before her freshman year. She was gone for a long time, and I began to wonder if something had happened. Something had indeed happened.

"What's wrong?" I asked with concern, seeing that Kim had been crying.

"The pastor won't marry us." Kim began to weep again.

"What? Why not?" I asked with bewilderment.

"He said he can't marry us because I'm a Christian and you're not," Kim said through her tears. "The pastor said if we got married, we would be unequally yoked. The Bible says Christians should not marry heathens. Light cannot mix with darkness, and I know he's right."

"What?! Who made that rule?!!" I exclaimed. "If he thinks I am going to become a Christian just to marry you, he's wrong. So what, he doesn't think I'm good enough? Did you tell him I'm the father of your child?"

"He knows." Kim was distraught. "He said God will take care of me if I trust in Him."

"Fine!" I shouted angrily. "Let God take care of you! The gall of some people!" I sped away in my car in utter disbelief.

At the time, I did not fully understand what was going on, and I became bitter towards the church. I thought a bunch of self-righteous prudes were trying to discredit every sacrifice I was making to do the responsible thing!

Kim contacted other pastors in the area only to receive the same response. This went on for nearly two weeks, and all the while, my animosity towards God and church people only deepened. It nearly severed Kim's and my relationship. Once again, I found myself on the verge of seeing my hopes elude my grasp.

Around the first of August, Kim had almost exhausted her list of local pastors; only one remained. He just happened to be pastoring the church across the street from where we were living—the Granite Falls Christian and Missionary Alliance. I didn't have a clue what the long name stood for, but at least it had the word Christian on the sign.

Kim used to attend the Christian and Missionary Alliance when she was a little girl, and she seemed comfortable approaching the pastor with our problem. After hearing our story, to our surprise, he agreed to marry us! He only had one request: Kim and I needed to meet with him for pre-marital counseling. I thought to myself that if this was going to provide Kim with some peace, then it was worth it.

When we entered the old, cinder block, musty-smelling building for our first counseling session, Pastor Steve Jones was waiting for us. He was warm, inviting, and had a smile on his face. To my surprise, he did not treat me like a heathen or a son of darkness. He actually seemed to care about our lives and patiently listened to our stories. When he asked permission to share with us something he was learning, I saw no threat in letting him speak.

He directed his questions towards me. "Danny, if you were to die tonight, do you know for certain that you would be in heaven with God?"

"Well, I don't think anyone can know for sure," I answered. "How could anyone know for certain if their good deeds outweigh their bad deeds? But I would like to think I would go to heaven. I was baptized as an infant in the Roman Catholic Church and was an altar boy for a couple years."

Pastor Steve was anxious to share more. "Danny, what if I told you that you *can* know for sure? Would it make a difference? How would it change your perspective on life? Look here. In 1 John 5:13, it states, "These things I have written to you who believe in the name of the Son of God, so that you may know that you have eternal life."

"Huh," I said, "that's pretty cool."

Pastor Steve followed up with another question, "Danny, if you died tonight and had to stand before God and He asked you, 'Why should I let you into My heaven?' what would you say?"

The question caught me off guard. "Well," I stammered, "I think I've been a pretty good person. I can think of a lot of people who have done worse things than I have. I've never really been one to put people down, and um... Oh! I have never killed anyone!"

Pastor Steve paused for a moment, then with excitement in his voice, he exclaimed, "Danny, I've got some good news to share with you. The greatest news you will ever hear!"

Pastor Steve proceeded to lay out God's plan of salvation using a presentation called Evangelism Explosion. Unbeknownst to me at the time, he was just learning how to communicate the gospel using this method, and I learned over two decades later that I was his first audience. It didn't matter. What he said resonated in my heart. Something, or rather Someone, was giving me cause to lower my defenses and listen intently to everything Pastor Steve had to say. He broke it down into seven points:

1. Heaven is a free gift; you can't earn it or deserve it.
2. Every person is a sinner with no hope of saving themselves. No matter how hard we try to be good, we can never erase the wrong we have done.
3. God is loving, holy and just, and He must punish sin.
4. Jesus Christ is God who took on human flesh. He came to be punished and die as our substitute. He did this in order to pay our fine—our sin penalty—in full.
5. On the third day, Jesus rose from the dead. This proved to the world that His perfect sacrifice was a sufficient payment that satisfied the demands of God's holy justice. Jesus took our sin upon Himself and, in exchange, gives us His righteousness.
6. Since God's righteous justice has been met, He can now rightfully offer forgiveness and pardon

all sins and offenses committed against Him. We receive forgiveness and eternal life when we repent and believe in what Jesus has accomplished on our behalf.

7. God provided this salvation in order to reconcile us to Himself and adopt us into His family as His very own.

"Wait a minute," I said. "I thought the Bible was a list of do's and don'ts. Are you saying that Jesus sacrificed Himself for me because God wants me to be His child?"

"Danny," Pastor Steve replied, "God wants to be your Father. He has been calling you by name your entire life. He is the Good Shepherd who is searching for His lost sheep, and He's gone to great lengths to bring you home."

Then Pastor Steve paused, looked into my eyes and asked, "Danny, is there any reason why you wouldn't want to respond to His invitation and receive the hope of salvation?"

I was surprised by the question. "Of course not! Who wouldn't want this?! It's almost too good to be true!"

"Then respond to Him," Pastor Steve urged me. "He's been listening, and He is waiting." I was eager to do just that, and Pastor Steve led me to pray and receive God's amazing gift of eternal life.

Afterward, with an even bigger grin than when we had first arrived, Pastor Steve gave me a hug and congratulated me, "Danny, welcome to the family of God!"

I felt like the prodigal son in Luke 15. After squandering away his entire inheritance and being reduced to feeding pigs when a famine hit the land, he finally came to his senses while contemplating sharing some slop with the hungry swine. He decided to go back to his father, confess his sin, beg for his father's mercy, and try to convince his father to take him back as a hired servant. The scripture states:

> *"He got right up and went home to his father.*
> *When he was still a long way off, his father saw*
> *him. His heart pounding, he ran out, embraced*
> *him, and kissed him. The son started his speech:*
> *'Father, I've sinned against God, I've sinned*
> *before you; I don't deserve to be called your son*
> *ever again.' But the father wasn't listening. He*

> *was calling to the servants, 'Quick. Bring a clean*
> *set of clothes and dress him. Put the family ring*
> *on his finger and sandals on his feet. Then get a*
> *grain-fed heifer and roast it. We're going to*
> *feast! We're going to have a wonderful time! My*
> *son is here—given up for dead and now alive!*
> *Given up for lost and now found!' And they*
> *began to have a wonderful time."*
> (Luke 15:20–24, MSG)

In similar fashion, I was stunned, ecstatic and overwhelmed by the Father's love for me. Even after all I had done—my rebelliousness, my disregard for His sovereignty, my cursing and taking His name in vain, and all my anger as I blamed Him for taking away what was most precious to me—He absorbed it all and still offered me kindness, grace and love.

I was taken aback to say the least! All my life, I had lived for nothing more than my kingdom to come and my will to be done, and it had never satisfied me. Now I was being invited to live for God's kingdom to come and for His will to be done. It felt right, like this was how it was really supposed to be!

Since that day, I have come to realize that life truly begins when we find ourselves back in the Father's embrace. It's the one place we are fully accepted and truly belong. God isn't calling us back to Himself to adhere to a set of doctrines and rules, and He's not waiting for us to clean up our act before we come home.

Instead, He calls us back to embrace us as His very own. He leaves the porch light on and stays up all night watching and waiting. Scanning the horizon, He calls each of us by name, and when He catches a glimpse of one of His filthy, penniless, wayward children on the road home, He comes to us. He comes running, and in His embrace, He whispers, "Welcome home, my child. You are wanted here." This is where CRAZY HOPE begins!

Kim re-dedicated her life to God that day as well, and our relationship began to blossom in new ways. I couldn't wait to start reading through the book of John with her as Pastor Steve suggested. Kim knew a lot about the Bible and was happy to answer all my questions. I knew something had been transformed at the core of my being when I suddenly had the desire to read. In the past, the Bible had never made sense to me, but now, it seemed to come alive!

I thank God that Pastor Steve not only had the courage to lead me to Christ, but that he also had the boldness to address something that could harm this new life I had found: my sin. After I had prayed to receive salvation, Pastor Steve said, "Danny, I know you will want to start doing things God's way now rather than your own way. So, do you think God would want you and Kim to keep living with each other before you are married?"

I knew the answer. "No," I replied.

"Danny, you have the opportunity to enter into your marriage with God's blessing. If you love Jesus, you will obey Him. If you allow the fear of the Lord to lead you into your marriage, then the love of the Lord and His blessing will abound in your marriage; and as a result, your trust and love for one another will grow stronger than ever."

Even though this was a radical and foreign concept to me, I agreed with everything Pastor Steve said. Not only that, but I had a strange joy following through with it. Something supernatural had happened in me. I actually wanted to obey God.

Kim and I both agreed that it would be best if she and Tanner, now two months old, moved back to her parents' house. Although it was inconvenient, we both wanted to do things God's way. Pastor Steve also warned me that I would be tempted and tested in my newfound faith. I didn't realize just how blatant the temptation would be.

The next day, Anthony and his brother stopped by to drop off a half rack of my favorite beer—ice-cold Miller Genuine Draft in bottles. They just happened to be thinking of me and wanted to swing by with the special delivery. I immediately thought of what Pastor Steve had said. Up until that point, I had been drinking steadily, and I knew I would start having withdrawals. This seemed like a test, looked like a test, and it sure felt like a test. I knew what I had to do.

"Thanks guys, but no thanks."

"What?" They were persistent. "No seriously, we know you and Kim have been going through some tough times, and we brought these over to put in your fridge. You can drink them later."

"No, you don't understand," I insisted. "I'm done with drinking. I became a Christian yesterday and I'm different now. I'm forgiven and I want to start living God's way." Anthony's eyes widened. They didn't know what to think, but they knew not to push it.

Kim and I finished delivering the last of her things to her parent's house, and I kissed her goodnight. In many ways, we had already been acting like a married couple while living together. This was a chance for us to back things up in order to do them right, and God began to bless us.

For the first time in a while, I found myself alone in my apartment, but I knew I was not truly alone. God was with me, and I could feel His presence and His pleasure. I began reading the book of John and started to become familiar with Jesus. Even though I knew very little, it seemed as though God were speaking directly to me through His Word. Later, I found out that this was normal. My Heavenly Father actually wanted me to know Him, just as He already knew me!

As I read, something started happening inside me that the Bible calls conviction. Conviction is when the Holy Spirit starts revealing things that are righteous— what God says is right, how things ought to be—and things that are unrighteous—what God says is wrong, how things ought not to be.

One of the first things God dealt with was my filthy mouth. Not using God's name in vain is in the top three of the Ten Commandments. *"You shall not take the name of the Lord your God in vain, for the Lord will not leave him unpunished who takes His name in vain"* (Exodus 20:7).

Knowing I had already broken the other nine commandments, it was disappointing to find out I had mastered the art of breaking the third as well, especially when I realized how much God hates it: *"The fear of the Lord is to hate evil; pride and arrogance and the evil way and the perverted mouth, I hate"* (Proverbs 8:13).

When I read about God's hatred of His name being taken in vain, I was horrified. However, each time I faced, admitted, and confessed my sin, it was God's approval that I felt, not His disapproval. It was as if He were saying, "Son, you're already forgiven. With you I am well pleased. Now go and sin no more."

It was God's kindness, patience, love and acceptance that really changed me. I was constantly being reminded that it was by God's grace that I had been saved through faith (Ephesians 2:8-10). Grace is a fascinating word that means "unearned favor." God chooses to treat us with kindness based on His character—not because we deserve it!

One night, I was flipping through television channels to find something pornographic. I had been introduced to pornography when I was twelve, and ever since then I had collected it on the walls of my room, under my mattress, and in my dresser drawers. No one had ever told me it was wrong; it just seemed like the thing to do.

Once again, the Holy Spirit convicted my heart, and I soon discovered that this was an "ought not." Uncontrolled lust is a result of the fall of man, not something God wants to characterize His children. It was only a healthy fear of God, along with His power, that gave me the desire and the ability to destroy the pornography I possessed. I began to practice turning my eyes away from that which was displeasing to my Heavenly Father.

God's acceptance, love and approval were beginning to form my new identity. I realized that, in the context of an intimate relationship with God, choosing to do what was right and desiring to please Him were expressions of my thankfulness for what Jesus Christ had already accomplished for me and of my love for Him. God was slowly beginning to change me into who He had created me to be in Him. The more I cooperated with His Spirit, the faster the process!

September 1, 1989. The big day had arrived and I was excited to finally be getting married. Kim and I chose to have an outdoor wedding in the backyard of her parents' home. The sky was overcast with dark clouds, but the temperature was perfect. Only family members were invited to the wedding ceremony, and everyone else was supposed to join us afterwards for the reception held at the community center. I don't think my friends got the memo because many of them showed up for both. Space in the side yard was limited, so most of them stood outside along the cyclone fence.

Kim looked absolutely gorgeous as she walked down the aisle. My heart leapt. I took her hand and held it in mine, and Pastor Steve began the ceremony. My brother Brian stood by as best man, and Kim's brother Jimmy was my groomsman. Kim's sister Tami was the maid of honor, and my sister Cheri was her bridesmaid. She promised not to steal my leg during the ceremony.

The highlight of the ceremony happened as I placed the ring on Kim's finger. Pastor Steve asked me if I had a token to symbolize my commitment in marriage, and I looked over at Brian who handed me the ring. I had just finished saying my vows and placing the ring on Kim's finger when, for the first time that day, the clouds let forth a clap of thunder! Startled, Pastor Steve exclaimed, "Well, it sounds like God approves!"

As the ceremony finished, Kim and I joined hands and made our way down the aisle. The second we stepped underneath the covered porch, the heavens released a torrential downpour. We kissed and knew for certain that God had brought us together.

God has a way of causing "all things to work together for good to those who love God, to those who are called according to *His* purpose" (Romans 8:28, emphasis mine).

Crazy Contemplation:

I now possessed CRAZY (wonderful, excellent, perfect) HOPE. It was just like Jesus described in one of His parables: when a man found treasure in a field, he joyfully went and sold everything he owned to buy the field (Matthew 13:44). My newfound HOPE was worth everything. When I compare the HOPE Christ gives with any other hope, there is no comparison. It makes me wonder why I waited so long to believe!

A few years ago, a Vietnam veteran named Bill was escorted into my office by one of his Marine friends named Dutch. Bill had always been a strong, courageous, intelligent, and very capable individual who had a rough and tough reputation around town. He was a survivalist who could live off the land and was combat-ready if the situation ever demanded it.

Bill was the only person I knew who could cast, machine, craft and assemble a long-range rifle with impeccable precision and accuracy without ever leaving the confines of his garage. Bill was a man's man, someone who'd had to overcome the negativity and brutal response he received from fellow Americans upon returning from the hellish horrors he had experienced in Vietnam.

Just a few hours before entering my office, Bill had received a death sentence from his doctor. Agent Orange, an herbicide and defoliant chemical used by the U.S. military as part of its chemical warfare program, had finally infiltrated his entire body, riddling it with cancer. Bill had just been told he had one month to live. When I met Bill that day, he sat across my desk fully clothed, yet wrapped in a blanket. He was trembling.

As I looked into Bill's eyes, asking God what I should say to him, Bill was sizing me up to discern whether or not I was worth listening to, whether I was someone he could trust. Deciding I was, he said, "This is the first time in my life I don't know what to do! I am terrified. I'm not ready to die."

"Bill, you don't realize it yet," I answered, "but you have just been given a wonderful gift."

"How can you say that?" Bill was taken aback. "I've been told I am going to die!"

"Bill, when I was fifteen, I nearly died in a car accident along with my girlfriend. I broke my back and lost my left leg. The tragedy and suffering I endured eventually helped me discover my great need for a savior. When I accepted Jesus Christ, I received a hope so great that I would rather give up all my limbs to know Christ, than have all my limbs, hopes, and dreams and not know Him." I testified, and Bill listened.

"Bill," I continued, "all your life you have been running from God and living for yourself. You have been placing your hope in anything and everything but God. Yet even though you have not wanted anything to do with God, He has been relentlessly pursuing you because He loves you." Bill was hanging on every word.

"Bill, God loves you deeply," I declared, "and He has mercifully brought you to this point of desperation. He has been patiently waiting for you to exhaust all your strength and energy and has allowed all your hopes to fail so you would realize that they are false and unable to satisfy or save. He has orchestrated all this so that you would finally sit, listen, and receive the hope of salvation He has been longing to give you. Because of that, you now find yourself in the most unlikely of situations... sitting across the desk from a pastor!"

God had divinely orchestrated that appointment with Bill. His heart was ready to receive the CRAZY HOPE of salvation that day, and it changed him from the inside out. His cancer progressed and his pain increased but so did his CRAZY HOPE. Bill refused to take any more pain medication in his final weeks. When asked why, he replied, "I want to be sober and clear-headed when I see my Savior face to face. If Jesus endured His pain for me with no medication, then I want to endure my pain for Him without medication."

I visited Bill in his home on a number of occasions over the following weeks. There were always caretakers present, whether family, friends, or other Vietnam veterans who were caring for and supporting a fellow comrade.

Before he died, Bill asked if he could be baptized. He explained why it was so important to him: "I want to be obedient to Jesus, and I want my life to be a testimony to others. I want people to know that if God can save me, He can save them too."

At Bill's request, I called a friend, Tim, and asked if he would help me baptize Bill. Dutch, Tim and I carried Bill upstairs in his wheelchair to the only bathtub in the house, and with great joy, Bill was baptized. One week later, he went home to the loving embrace of his Savior and King.

Why do I tell you Bill's story? Because Bill asked me to tell his story.

Bill had lived a very rebellious life, and the horrors he had experienced in Vietnam caused him to sink even further into depravity. As a result, Bill ran and hid from God for almost his entire life. The atrocities he had committed caused him to believe he was beyond saving. Up until his last month on earth, he wanted nothing to do with God because he believed God wanted nothing to do with him. Nothing could have been further from the truth.

Bill finally realized that this was a lie from the pit of hell—only Satan could conjure up such a pernicious lie. His aim is to isolate and alienate us from God. His goal has always been to leave us discouraged and hopeless.

Let me make this perfectly clear: *no one is beyond saving.*

To believe such a thing is to call God a liar and to devalue the sacrifice of Christ. God declares that His Son's blood is sufficient to wash away ALL sin. He publicly declared that Christ's sacrifice was sufficient when He raised His Son from the dead!

So, I have to ask you, "If you died tonight and stood before God, and He asked you, 'Why should I let you into My heavenly kingdom?' what would you say?"

Your answer reveals what kind of crazy hope you possess. It shows who or what you are trusting in to obtain eternal life. It also reveals something about your true identity, namely, to whom you ultimately belong. Jesus said there are only two possible answers: we either belong to the Father in Heaven or to the father of lies.

If you are unsure how to answer the question of why God should let you into His kingdom, I encourage you to go back and read my conversation with Pastor Steve. Ask God to reveal any crazy false hopes you might still be holding onto; and when He does, release your grip and surrender them to Him. I can guarantee that Abba Father will replace those false hopes with a HOPE that is eternal and priceless.

[Note to all military veterans: When Bill stepped into my office, I was privileged to be invited into a very tight-knit community of veterans. There was something unique and special about the bond of brotherhood I observed in Bill's home. Army, Navy, Air Force, and Marines were all represented. It was obvious that as former comrades you continue to have one another's backs.

I know many of you have experienced the worst side of humanity, and for a period of time, war, violence, and death were the norm; and that temporary period of time ended up changing you permanently. PTSD still haunts some of you to this day, and many of you carry a burden that often feels unbearable. Although you may not have died in battle for your friends, I know you were willing, and that says a lot about you. Jesus said, "Greater love has no one than this, that one lay down his life for his friends" (John 15:13).

Whether you have a group of comrades you spend time with, or whether you are all alone, my prayer is that you would know you are never alone. None of us is beyond God's reach, and He has not given up in His pursuit of you. The Son of God, who sacrificed His life for you, offers His promise of HOPE and salvation to anyone willing to respond to His invitation and call:

> *"Come to Me, all who are weary and heavy-laden, and I will give you rest. Take My yoke upon you and learn from Me, for I am gentle and humble in heart, and you will find rest for your souls. For My yoke is easy and My burden is light." (Matthew 11:28–30)*

"For God so loved the world that he gave his one and only Son, that whoever believes in him shall not perish but have eternal life. For God did not send his Son into the world to condemn the world, but to save the world through him."
(John 3:16–17)

As with the first responders I addressed earlier, you have my deepest honor and respect. Thank you for your personal sacrifice and service to our country.]

CHAPTER 12

with great enthusiasm or energy; to an extreme:
Living with CRAZY HOPE

For the second time in my life, everything changed: my actions, attitude, perspective, desires and, of course, my definition of crazy hope. I now possessed CRAZY—wonderful, excellent, perfect—HOPE! Three characteristics of CRAZY HOPE manifest themselves in someone who possesses it:

I. CRAZY HOPE COMPELS: It compels us to want to give it to others.

II. CRAZY HOPE PERSEVERES: It actually increases when trials, tribulations, persecution, suffering, pain, and disappointment come.

III. CRAZY HOPE ANCHORS: It alone possesses the capability to anchor us through the fiercest storms of life.

I) *CRAZY HOPE COMPELS*

After personally experiencing the eradication of my cancerous sin when I received Jesus as my Lord and Savior, I was compelled to make this CRAZY HOPE known to others!

So, with great zeal, I started with my friends and family. It didn't go over very well. From their reactions, you would've thought I was trying to finagle them into a multi-level marketing scam. They either didn't want to hear about it, or they were entirely indifferent. It didn't make sense to me. I couldn't understand why people didn't want the antidote to the poison of sin.

I soon discovered a common thread. Most people I talked with didn't believe they needed the hope of salvation. Their responses varied but were all basically the same:

"I'm happy for you, Danny. It's just not for me."

"No thanks, I have my own way of believing in God."

"Oh Danny, you're just excited. Give it some time and it will wear off."

I was dumbfounded! Jesus had changed and healed me, and I knew He would do the same for them if they just believed. But then I remembered that for eighteen years of my life, I had rejected the salvation God offered in the same way.

I figured that since I couldn't get through to them, I needed to take them to the professional—Pastor Steve. So, I set up multiple appointments where Pastor Steve could convince all my family and friends.

Observing my dilemma, Pastor Steve wisely took me under his wing and taught me how to effectively and clearly communicate the good news of the hope of salvation in Christ. This not only helped me articulate the greatest news a person can hear, but it also helped me better understand the length and width and height and depth of this new love and hope I possessed.

I realized one of the main reasons people weren't interested in salvation was because I never told them about their need for it. I always wanted to cut straight to the good news. In other words, I tried to offer them the solution without first pointing out their cancerous sin problem. I would say, "Christ died on the cross for you, and He wants to save you!" But they didn't know why they needed saving.

It's no wonder the typical response was, "Save me from what? I am doing just fine. I don't need to live with a crutch."

Henry came over to the house one day and I had the privilege of sharing with him what had happened to me. In a way, Henry was following in my footsteps. He had gotten his girlfriend pregnant, they got married the day after we did, and his wife had just given birth to their son whom they ended up naming Cody.

As I talked with Henry, instead of starting with the good news of the gospel, I first told him about the bad news: his cancerous sin problem that would end his life with eternal death.

Thankfully, God had already been working on Henry's heart. He knew he had sinned and offended Holy God, and he already believed a judgment day was coming. As a result, I was able to offer him the antidote—salvation through Christ—and he drank it down. One of my best friends was now healed and saved!

As I waited for my lawyers to finalize the three million dollar lawsuit with the automobile maker, I began my first job at Boeing correcting airplane wiring diagrams and schematics. Simply stated, I assigned a number to each change made by a certified engineer. It was a bunch of busy work and was one of the first departments to go when Boeing skimmed some fat off its budget in 1991.

Ultimately, it didn't really matter what I was doing. Introducing people to Jesus was my real work, and Boeing was a huge mission field! I sat at a desk surrounded by six other people. Every month, we rotated spots, and I would find myself sitting next to six new people. It was awesome! Some came to Christ; most were indifferent; and only a few were hostile.

God also gave me a newfound love for my dad, and I began reaching out to him. I truly believed that Jesus could bring him the hope, peace, and contentment he'd always been searching for. However, things didn't go quite like I expected, and I saw a part of my dad I never knew existed. This was a critical time for me. It's when I began to experience how CRAZY HOPE perseveres.

II) CRAZY HOPE PERSEVERES

My dad was now living alone in a small, dark, dreary apartment in Everett. He was no longer allowed to own a car, so Kim and I tried to assist him in matters of need.

During our visits, I always felt led to share with him the truths I was learning about God. Our discussions reminded me of the conversation Jesus had with a Pharisee named Nicodemus in the third chapter of John. There, Jesus told Nicodemus, *"Unless you are born again [or born from above] you will not enter into the Kingdom of God"* (John 3:3).

Neither Nicodemus nor my dad had a clue what it meant to be born again. Both of them were trusting in their religious ways and superstitions. For Nicodemus, salvation came through his Jewish heritage, religious customs, and ceremonial washings. For my dad, salvation came through the Roman Catholic Church, the sacraments, and infant baptism.

When Jesus declared, "You must be born again," He cut the legs out from under all belief systems that claim righteousness can be achieved through human effort or merit. Not wanting to leave Nicodemus legless, Jesus reminded him of an Old Testament story Nicodemus most likely had memorized. It's found in Numbers 21:4-9.

As they left Mount Hor, the nation of Israel grew impatient and began grumbling and speaking out against God and Moses. As punishment, God sent fiery serpents among the people. Whoever was bitten by one of those serpents soon died. After many had perished, the people went to Moses and said, *"We have sinned, because we have spoken against the LORD and you; intercede with the Lord, that He may remove the serpents from us"* (Numbers 21:6).

Moses interceded for the people; however, God didn't take away the serpents. Instead, God had Moses make a bronze serpent and place it on top of a pole. God said, *"It shall come about, that everyone who is bitten, when he looks at the bronze serpent, he will live"* (Numbers 21:8).

As Jesus spoke with Nicodemus centuries later, He looked him in the eye and made one of the greatest statements in all of history:

"As Moses lifted up the serpent in the wilderness, even so must the Son of Man be lifted up; so that whoever believes will in Him have eternal life.

For God so loved the world, that He gave His only
begotten Son, that whoever believes in Him shall
not perish, but have eternal life. For God did not
send the Son into the world to judge the world,
but that the world might be saved through Him."
(John 3:14–17)

Jesus used this illustration to make something crystal clear to all the people like Nicodemus in the world: "You've been bitten by the serpent of serpents, and his venom of evil and sin runs through your veins. No matter what you do on the outside, you cannot change what is on the inside. You need an outside source, an intervention, a miracle antidote. I Am the Antidote. Look at Me, believe in Me, trust in Me, and you will be born again, healed, and saved!"

This was a tough pill for Nicodemus to swallow and for my dad as well. Both would have to admit that all their moral efforts had been worthless. In essence, Jesus was saying, "All the sacrifices, confessions, sacraments, Hail Mary's and washings; all the rule keeping, law abiding, tithe offering and confessions have not gotten you any closer to righteousness than the day you began. Your cancerous sin defiles you, defines you, and disqualifies you. But this is why I came: to be placed on top of a pole—the cross—to represent your sin. After I suffer the punishment and wrath your sins deserve, I will have the ability and right to give you My forgiveness, My Spirit, My life, and My righteousness. If you believe and trust in Me, you will be born again!"

Jesus knew our plight. He didn't come to make bad people good; He came to make dead people alive. He came to be our Substitute, to be our Savior.

> *"For the wages of sin is death, BUT the free gift*
> *of God is eternal life in Christ Jesus our Lord."*
> *(Romans 6:23, emphasis mine)*

My dad wrestled with these truths for months, and he took it out on me. He got angry, felt belittled, and accused me of judging him. At times, I felt like he would have disowned me if it were possible. So, Kim and I prayed, and God began to work.

After months of turmoil, I got a call from my dad one night. He sounded different. With peace and calm in his voice, he said, "Danny, you know that peace you have been talking about? I finally have it! I believe in Jesus!"

We had a great conversation that night. He told me that after our most recent discussion, he decided to open up the book of Matthew. As he read Matthew's account of the crucifixion of Christ, tears filled his eyes, God spoke to his heart, and by the time he finished, he was a new man. My dad was born again! I was ecstatic! I praised God for opening up my dad's heart to receive CRAZY HOPE.

I was looking forward to rejoicing with my dad in person; however, before I had the chance, tragedy struck. A few days after his phone call, I received a call from a police officer. The officer said, "While getting on a bus in Everett, your dad collapsed and was rushed to the ER."

Kim and I rushed to the hospital. When I saw my dad, his head was swollen to twice its normal size. The doctor informed us that he had a brain aneurysm and that there was nothing they could do. My dad never did regain consciousness, and within a matter of hours, he was gone.

My dad's brain aneurysm caught all of us off guard; however, his phone call was a gift. When he told me he had finally received the peace I had so desperately been trying to convince him existed, it was a game changer. Even death is unable to destroy CRAZY HOPE; it merely ushers us in to finally meet the One who *is* our HOPE.

Maybe my dad was right. Maybe retirement *does* ultimately produce contentment. Not retirement from a job but retirement from this earthly existence—when we are finally home, where Jesus wipes away every tear and His embrace says it all: "You are welcome here."

Before I move on, I want to emphasize something very important. I mentioned that my dad and I had many conversations. Let me tell you, they were tough. The evil one had a stronghold in my dad's life, and he wasn't about to let go. The Apostle Paul wrote to Timothy explaining this phenomenon:

> *The Lord's bond-servant must not be quarrelsome, but be kind to all, able to teach, patient when wronged, with gentleness correcting those who are in opposition, if perhaps God may grant them repentance leading to the knowledge of the truth, and they may come to their senses and escape from the snare of the devil, having been held captive by him to do his will. (2 Timothy 2:24–26)*

I write this because Christians need to be reminded of what we are up against. It is easy to get discouraged when those we love reject or even attack us. If we fail to remember that they are not attacking us but Jesus Christ, we may find it tempting to quit.

We need to remember that we are simply the Lord's bondservants seeking to be faithful ambassadors. If we will faithfully do our part, we can trust that God will do His. People are being ensnared and held captive by sin. If we can remember their true spiritual state, it will give us the compassion and boldness to help those who want to escape. Never lose HOPE!

III) CRAZY HOPE ANCHORS

You know that you have CRAZY HOPE when you find yourself still anchored and secure when the trials and storms of life hit.

On March 15, 1991, God blessed Kim and I with our second child, a beautiful baby girl we named Christa Michelle. Tanner and Christa were bosom buddies from day one.

As time went on, we began to plan for our future and decided it would be best if Kim stayed home to raise our children. We trusted that God would provide for us financially. We also made the decision to homeschool our children so they would have a solid foundation in their faith in Christ before we sent them off into the world. These decisions and sacrifices were about to be tested.

I had not heard much from the lawyer who was handling the lawsuit against the automobile maker. So when he called one day out of the blue, it was quite a surprise. The conversation did not go well.

The lawyer told me that he had discussed my situation with the corporate lawyers, and they had made a proposal. "Danny," the lawyer explained, "the automobile company said that if we tried to take them to court, they would run us out of money before we could ever get there. They did make an offer, however. They agreed to pay the sum of one hundred fifty thousand dollars. I think it is your only option and you should take it."

I was shocked! For years, I had been depending on this money as a source of income; yet, for some reason, I wasn't devastated. In a strange way, God had been preparing my heart ahead of time to receive this news, and for the first time, I realized I no longer felt the need to be a millionaire. My CRAZY HOPE and security were no longer placed there. They were now placed in Someone greater—Someone who owned the cattle on a thousand hills, Someone who owned all things. Somehow, I knew God would take care of us and provide for all our needs.

Having no other alternative, we decided to take the offer; and after the lawyer had taken a third of the settlement, that chapter of my life was finally closed.

We put all the money towards buying a house, which turned out to be a wise investment. Over the years, God has always provided just what we need. The settlement gave us just enough for Kim to stay home and for us to continue depending on God's faithful provision.

As a new believer, Henry was just beginning to discover God's faithfulness as well. He was growing in his faith and reading through the New Testament. He especially loved the book of Acts. However, he was struggling in his new marriage. So, when his wife flew down to California with their baby to visit relatives, we had him over for a barbeque. Knowing he was a bit down, Kim and I tried to keep things upbeat and positive.

After some good conversation and a few laughs, Henry left. I never saw him again. I did not realize the spiritual battle that was raging around him, and I failed to discern the turmoil that was growing within him.

That night, Henry allowed darkness to get the upper hand. After another argument over the phone with his wife, he sat alone at home with darkened thoughts and feelings of despair. He positioned a chair facing the front entrance and sat down with a loaded shotgun in his hand. To this day, I wonder why he pulled the trigger.

In the morning, Anthony drove over to Henry's house to see how he was doing. Oddly, the front door was unlocked. As he opened the door, Anthony saw the gruesome after-effects of Henry's suicide. In his darkest hour, Henry had shot himself in the head.

In panic and shock, Anthony called me to report what he'd found. I couldn't believe it! I quickly jumped in my car and drove out to Henry's place, seething with anger. This was a terrible prank... I hoped it was a terrible prank.

When I got there, Anthony would not let me enter the house, shielding me from what he had seen. To this day, he has vivid memories of that horrific morning. As police arrived on scene, I realized it was not a prank. This was really happening.

Afterwards, many of my former classmates gathered together, trying to make sense of what had happened. Henry was strong, capable, and talented. He came from a good, solid family that cared about him, and he had so much going for him. So why would he throw his life away?

Towards the end of our time together, we seemed to have more questions than when we arrived. However, before we went our separate ways, I had the opportunity to share about Henry's newfound faith and hope in Christ.

Henry had failed to see how Christ could help him persevere through his moment of anguish, but that did not negate the fact that he had already entrusted his soul to his merciful Savior and Lord. In other words, he still trusted in Jesus for his salvation, even though he had failed to trust Jesus to get him through the trial.

I am convinced that Henry knew where he was going and, in a moment of selfishness, chose instant relief over persevering through pain. Suicide is not the unforgivable sin. Refusing to believe in and receive God's promise of salvation is.

Before we went our separate ways that day, I prayed for all of my former classmates as well as for Henry's family. This was the first time many of them had seen me since I surrendered my life to Christ.

A week later, we gathered together once again at the Christian and Missionary Alliance church for Henry's memorial service. There was standing room only. It was as if the entire town of Granite Falls had gathered together.

Pastor Steve Jones had moved with his family to teach Evangelism Explosion in Illinois, and a new pastor had just arrived. Pastor Keith Crane was present with his young family to help minister during this tragic time. I was thankful he was there.

I had the opportunity to speak at Henry's service, and I shared some funny experiences we'd had together; but my greatest desire was to somehow impart CRAZY

HOPE and lead this hurting community to the hidden treasure in the field.

Afterward, several people thanked me for sharing and said they were encouraged by my testimony. Seeds were planted that day, one of which soon took root in Anthony's heart. When he finally surrendered his life to Christ, we rejoiced greatly! Since that day, Anthony and his lovely wife have taken multiple mission trips to spread the love of Jesus around the world.

In many ways, I was just beginning to realize and experience that my CRAZY HOPE in Christ would anchor me through the toughest of times; but, unlike Henry, I had to keep my eyes fixed on Jesus (Hebrews 12:1-3). If we fail to keep our eyes on Him through the trials of life, the pain we experience in this fleeting world could prove to be our undoing. It wasn't long before I would be thoroughly tested as well.

As time went on, Kim and I were blessed with two more children: Jacob Daniel was born in 1995 and Victoria Joy in 1998. God definitely had a sense of humor proving the doctors wrong! This whole time, Kim homeschooled our children, and even with only one modest income, God always provided just what we needed.

I had sensed God calling me into ministry right after I was saved. As a result, I viewed each of my jobs as a mission field. As I shared my testimony with my coworkers, I would often be told that I should become a minister; however, I was very content being on the front lines. I thrived on every opportunity I had to convey CRAZY HOPE to those who had not yet received it, and I had the privilege of leading many to Christ.

In 1997, my health began to go downhill. My leg and back began giving me trouble. The bottom of my stump developed an ulcer, and because I had no curvature in my spine, my back began to throb with chronic pain.

At the time, I was a journeyman meat cutter in a prominent supermarket. For months, I was unable to walk back to the meat department without leaning on a shopping cart, and once I got back there, I would use the countertops to get myself around. It was the first time since recovering from my accident that my limitations became all-encompassing.

It became apparent that if I did not find some kind of relief, I would have to quit my job. Unfortunately, instead of turning to Christ for wisdom and direction, I turned to my doctor and was introduced to narcotics.

At first, the painkillers seemed to be the answer. They perked me up and allowed me to keep going. But as time went on, my pain and the amount of narcotics I needed increased. Without realizing it, I was beginning to dig myself into a hole—and this was only the beginning.

Fortunately, I was working at a slower-paced store that was close to home. But my situation went from bad to worse when my manager called me into his office out of the blue and said, "Dan, you are being transferred to the Edmonds meat department. Don from the Everett store is butting heads with his manager and they are sending him here."

This was shocking news! It seemed that Don was actually getting rewarded for his bad attitude. He was being moved to a slower-paced store closer to home, and I was being sent to one of the highest volume stores twice as far from home! I prayed that God would right this wrong, but His answer was no.

My time at the Edmonds store was brutal. Not only was I constantly in pain, but I was now working for a manager who delighted in cracking the whip and was never pleased.

Furthermore, after sharing my testimony with the meat cutters in Edmonds, I experienced persecution for the first time. They were relentless. Once, a man even pulled out one of his knives in a state of rage and threatened me! I often wept as I drove the long commute home. I cried out to God wondering why things were so difficult.

Thankfully, as the months went by, my coworkers in the meat department began to soften and began asking me questions about my faith. One gave his life to Christ, and I could tell God was working in the hearts of others, including my manager and the man who had pulled his knife on me.

Unfortunately, during this time, my body was deteriorating and so was my prayer life. Without realizing it, I began slipping into depression.

Every morning involved the same grueling process. With my back sore and stiff, it was difficult to sit up in bed. When I was finally upright, I needed to muster up the courage to step into my artificial limb. It felt like lowering my stump onto knives. After two or three hours, my leg would finally become numb which allowed the pain in my back to return with a fury.

The doctor continued to increase my narcotics, and migraines were added to my list of suffering. Yet instead of turning to Christ for guidance and wisdom, I kept looking to other things to get me out from under this suffocating trial. Once again, I placed my hope in the medical field.

In 1998, I had revision surgery on my stump because the initial amputation in 1986 had been unsuccessful. The inner thigh muscle that was stretched around the end had torn away leaving nothing but skin and bone and causing ulcers and all kinds of problems.

The physician amputated two-and-a-half more inches and reattached the muscle. After waking up from surgery, it felt like my leg was on fire, but there was little the doctors could do given the amount of narcotics I was taking at the time. It was a horrific experience. Even worse, within six months, the muscle ripped away from the bone again, and I was back to square one. After this, I just learned to live with it.

At the beginning of 1999, I had the Harrington Rods removed from my spine in an attempt to alleviate some of the pain in my back. This painful surgery was also unsuccessful, and the removal of the rods did nothing to bring pain relief. My depression deepened.

Since pain medicine and surgeries weren't helping, I placed my hope in becoming a meat manager. This, I thought, would cause me less physical strain and reduce the amount of time I was on my feet; however, whenever management positions opened up, they were given to others with less experience but more shrewdness in dealing with corporate managers.

By this time, my anxiety level was maxed out and I started becoming paranoid. I kept telling myself, "I have to keep going. How can I quit my job with a wife and four children at home depending on me?"

My last ditch effort was to try and sell our home and downsize. That would allow me to work less. But our home sat on the market for months with little to no activity.

All my efforts were now exhausted. Everything I had placed my hope in to get me out from under this trial had been met with slammed doors. I was now clinically depressed.

A speaker at a conference I attended around this time gave a description of clinical depression. He said it was like being tied up, hung upside down, placed in a black plastic bag, and then lowered into a never-ending vat of oil. What a great description. Clinical depression is experiencing darkness, helplessness and suffocation with no way of escape, no joy, and no hope. I now have a greater understanding of why some would choose suicide.

As I drove home from yet another agonizing day at work, I had an anxiety attack and changed course with the intent of checking myself into the hospital's mental ward. Thankfully, the attack partially lifted, and I had second thoughts. I decided to delay it one more day and discuss my plan to admit myself with Kim.

I pulled into our driveway, literally crawled out of the car, and slowly made my way into the house and out to the back porch. I sat with my face in my hands and sobbed. When Kim saw me, she quickly made her way out to comfort me. "Kim," I cried, "I can't do it anymore! I can't keep going like this! I have exhausted every avenue and there is nowhere else to turn!"

In that moment, Kim opened up her Bible and turned to Philippians 4:4-7. "Dan," she urged me, "please read this. I think it will encourage you."

I took the Bible from her hand and began to read:

Rejoice in the Lord always; again I will say, rejoice! Let your gentle spirit be known to all men. The Lord is near. Be anxious for nothing, but in everything by prayer and supplication with thanksgiving let your requests be made known to God. And the peace of God, which surpasses all comprehension, will guard your hearts and your minds in Christ Jesus. (Philippians 4:4–7)

As I read, God spoke to my heart: "Dan, when is the last time you rejoiced in Me or remembered that I am near? You have been anxious about everything. When is the last time you prayed or gave supplication with thanksgiving? When is the last time you let your requests be made known to Me? Now you know why My peace is not guarding your heart and your mind. Dan... it's time to believe and place your hope in Me alone!"

I was deeply convicted and overwhelmed. It felt like being hit over the head with a two-by-four! For the first time in two years, it dawned on me that I was making all my decisions based on fear and not faith. I was so terrified of giving in to my limitations that I had lost sight of the limitless power and hope that I already possessed in Christ.

As a result, I had placed my hope in everything I could think of to deliver me out of the trial instead of asking the questions that would have given me the right perspective and provided hope in the midst of the trial:

- God, what are You trying to teach me?
- What does my response reveal about my trust in You?
- How do You want me to respond?
- Is there a lie I am believing?
- What truth do I need to start believing?
- God, what is your desire and will for my life?

God was already beginning to provide the answers. If I had asked these questions in 1997, I could have avoided a whole lot of pain and suffering; but now that God had my attention, I was eager to listen. I would soon discover that He was allowing this trial in my life for a very good reason.

Immediately after this encounter with God, I vowed to begin intentionally trusting God's Word regardless of how I felt. I made a new resolution to take the truth I knew in my head and begin believing it in my heart. This is ultimately how I climbed out of my depression.

Falling into depression had been a slow process, and climbing out was just as slow. I started journaling and writing out my "prayers and supplications with thanksgiving" and rejoicing in the Lord. One by one, God answered every prayer down to the minutest detail!

That same night, I sensed God calling me to quit my job and to begin trusting Him as the Provider. So the next day, I sat down with my store manager to resign. To my surprise, he tried to convince me to stay by offering me the meat manager position I had been wanting at the store closest to home! However, I knew it was a test and politely turned down the offer. I sensed God saying, "I could have given you that position all along, but it is not what I have called you to."

In 2000, I filled out paperwork to receive Social Security Disability benefits, and God allowed it to be approved without any resistance or need for appeal.

Now that I had health insurance, I made an appointment with a top-notch surgeon to see if there was anything that could be done for my back.

Thankfully, God led me to a surgeon who had just developed a new procedure for my condition. Although it wouldn't be a permanent fix, he projected at least ten years of relief and after that the pain would move into my pelvic region. His prediction would prove to be correct. Unfortunately, once your spine is fused, all surgical options are exhausted and you have to live with the pain.

At the beginning of 2002, I underwent the operation to reshape and add curvature back to my spine. The surgeon cut a wedge in the middle of my spinal fusion, which he described like the wedge someone makes to chop down a tree. After the wedge was taken out, he then closed the space and fused the remainder of my spine to my pelvis. My spine now has a thirty-six degree curvature, and I lost an inch and a half in height. It was worth it.

This surgery was extremely successful; however, the recovery was intolerable. When I awoke from surgery, I literally felt no pain because of the epidural in my spine.

But during the shift change, the new nurse failed to feed the epidural, and at 3am I woke up into a nightmare with no epidural and no pain medication. I felt every part of the surgery. "Help!" I screamed. "I need help!"

When the nurse arrived, she saw my death grip on the bed rail and noticed that my epidural had run out. "Can you give me a shot?" I pleaded.

She went to check and came back with the answer, "Not until the doctor comes in."

"When will that be? Is he on his way?" I pleaded.

"No, he will come at 7am."

I couldn't believe it. I felt like I was being tortured as I held onto the bed rail for the next four hours. I don't know how I endured that night; but later on, a lady from church informed me that people had been praying for my surgery. God had woken her up at 3am that night, and she had prayed until morning.

When the surgeon finally entered my room, he was saddened to hear what had happened during the night and quickly got me some pain medication. Once I was comfortable, he was eager to tell me something that had happened during surgery. "The surgery went well—

incredibly well!" he said. "I've never experienced this before, but it was like someone was guiding my hands during the entire procedure!" I knew this was confirmation that God was taking care of me even through suffering.

Over the next five years, God restored my joy and hope. He provided miraculously for me and my family, and I sensed Him saying, "It's not your job that has ever provided for you. I alone have been providing for all your needs."

During this time, God gave me new vision and direction. At the end of 2002, I sensed Him reviving my call to full-time ministry, and I started seminary with the Christian and Missionary Alliance. Over the next few years, I had multiple opportunities to preach and teach.

God gave me further confirmation during this time through two random encounters I had with other Christians who were going through similar circumstances. It was like hearing my story being told back to me. At first, they too had resisted God's call on their lives. One man had his calf muscles harden up and could no longer continue working in construction. The other was bound to a wheelchair because of some mysterious ailment. Both of these men went on to pursue God's call and experience the joy of the Lord in their ministries to this day.

In 2004, our family felt led to adopt a 5-year-old boy from the foster system. We were informed that his biological father was not safe and that we should seek to have his name changed. Samuel Joseph became our fifth and final addition to the family.

In 2005, I finished seminary and God began to reveal more of His perfectly orchestrated plan. I had always assumed that I would become the assistant pastor of the C&MA church I was a part of, but God had other plans and opened up a very unexpected door.

The Community Bible Church in Granite Falls asked if I would become their pastor. The church was about ready to close its doors after searching for a pastor for over a year and a half. Sensing God's leading, I began to pray with the C&MA leadership.

If I took this pastoral position, I would have to give up my Social Security Disability Insurance as well as my meat cutter disability pension. At first, I tried to convince another Christian brother who had just finished seminary to take the position. However, God laid the Community Bible Church on my heart to such an extent that it was almost impossible for me to say no.

God reminded me of how He had provided for my family over the last five years, and He gave me the faith to believe He would continue to do so. Confident of this, I took the position.

On March 1, 2005, I became the pastor of the Community Bible Church. It was obvious that God had led me there. Within seven years, He had revived this dying church of thirty people and increased it to over one hundred and fifty. God not only brought new life, but He also increased the depth of our love for one another and for the community. To this day, it is a growing and thriving congregation spreading CRAZY HOPE throughout the region and beyond!

Through these experiences and many others, I have learned that CRAZY HOPE anchors us even when life seems to be crumbling all around. Even when all other hopes fail, CRAZY HOPE in Christ endures. Throughout this time, I learned how to fix my eyes on Jesus alone as my source of hope; and I discovered that as long as our eyes are fixed on Him, nothing is able to derail us—nothing.

Time and again, the treasure I now possess has proven to neither falter nor fade. It seems that the greater the pain, the greater its comfort; the greater the turmoil, the greater its peace; the greater the darkness, the brighter its light. CRAZY HOPE COMPELS us to love the unlovable; CRAZY HOPE PERSEVERES through the severest trials; and CRAZY HOPE ANCHORS us to Christ, the Rock of all ages. CRAZY HOPE not only restores our true identity, it is how God leads us home.

Crazy Contemplation:

CRAZY HOPE changes lives! It allows you to live your life with "great enthusiasm or energy; to an extreme." It is the narrow way that leads to life. CRAZY HOPE restores your true purpose and begins the process of changing you into the fullness of who God has created you to be.

- There is great security in knowing you have been created for an intimate love relationship with our Heavenly Father.
- There is true satisfaction when you understand that you are fully accepted and belong to the King, have been adopted as His child, and are made heir to His throne.

- There is incredible significance and worth when you realize that you are uniquely created to bring eternal glory to God Almighty!
- There is something extremely liberating in knowing that the Creator and Sustainer of the universe is for you, not against you.
- There is enormous excitement when God places His Spirit and power within you to accomplish His eternal purpose and will.
- There is great purpose in knowing you are here to make a name for God and not yourself.
- There is rich meaning to life when you know God's redemptive plan is to ultimately restore and make all things new!

When we seek hope apart from God, is it any wonder security and contentment elude us? We were made to know and enjoy our Creator above all else. This is where our true identity lies.

However, many people, including myself, get hung up on the question, "If God is good, then why all the pain and suffering in the world?" After receiving CRAZY HOPE, I came to better understand the answer.

At the beginning of mankind's existence, we rebelled against our Creator. Afterward, God allowed thorns and thistles to grow as part of the curse brought on by our rebellion (Genesis 3:17-19). God knew that if pain, toil, sweat, suffering and death were not part of the curse, we would attempt to make a heaven of our life on earth apart from Him. But this is not how the Creator originally designed things to be; it's not how life was meant to be or how it ought to be.

Why does God allow all the disappointment, rejection, suffering, betrayal, violence, loss and death in our lives? Could it be that pain and suffering are like plows designed to break up the hardened, fallow soil in our hearts? Apart from pain and suffering, agony and death, would our hearts ever be open to receive the seed of the gospel containing CRAZY HOPE?

What if our greatest disappointment could actually become the catalyst leading to our greatest blessing?

What if God strips away our false hopes in order to give us true hope?

In light of eternity and all that is at stake, wouldn't that be the most loving thing God could do?

REWRITING MY CHAPTERS

When my false crazy hopes were replaced with true CRAZY HOPE, the chapter titles of my life were forever changed:

1. CRAZY HOPE makes sense of the senseless and reveals all that is certain, practical, and sound; it exposes what is real, true, and everlasting.

2. CRAZY HOPE in Christ has become the main thing I am intensely enthusiastic and passionately excited about. He is the only One worthy of all my adoration and worship.

3. CRAZY HOPE invites me into the most intimate relationship known to man—to be enamored of and infatuated with the Maker, Lover, Shepherd, and Guardian of my soul.

4. CRAZY HOPE transcends every circumstance, experience, or tragedy and remains unchanged when the casual turns to chaos.

5. CRAZY HOPE is the constant, unseen reality that pervades all of life; it provides answers when life is interrupted by chaos.

6. CRAZY HOPE replaces anxiety with faith and impatience with trust.

7. CRAZY HOPE loosens the bonds of anger and fills my heart with thankfulness.

8. CRAZY HOPE transforms my recklessness into righteousness.

9. CRAZY HOPE is unusually bizarre and almost scandalous! While we were yet sinners and enemies of God, Christ died for us (Romans 5:7-8)! Holy God humbling Himself to serve and give His life as a ransom in order to offer forgiveness to the unforgivable and grace to the undeserving? Overwhelming!

10. CRAZY HOPE replaced my father's suicidal pursuits with salvation's peace!

11. CRAZY HOPE is wonderful, excellent, and perfect because it finds its source in the wonderful Counselor, excellent Redeemer, and perfect Savior. It is His work, His sufficiency, His power and all for His glory!

12. CRAZY HOPE inspires great, extreme enthusiasm because it begins the process of restoring us to our original glorified state and allows us to discover our true, eternal identity within the confines of a perfectly reconciled relationship with our Creator.

Our True Identity

"Therefore, since we have been made right in God's sight by faith, we have peace with God because of what Jesus Christ our Lord has done for us. Because of our faith, Christ has brought us into this place of undeserved privilege where we now stand, and we confidently and joyfully look forward to sharing God's glory. We can rejoice, too, when we run into problems and trials, for we know that they help us develop endurance. And endurance develops strength of character, and character strengthens our confident hope of salvation. And this hope will not lead to disappointment. For we know how dearly God loves us, because He has given us the Holy Spirit to fill our hearts with His love."
(Romans 5:1–5, NLT)

God's word is powerful! In the beginning, God spoke and all things were created. Then, God gave His written word to reveal His nature and character. At the right time, the Word of God became flesh and dwelt among us. Today, God's word is changing the lives of those who hear it and respond. It transforms believers into new creations, bringing them into fellowship with God the Father and with the Word of God—Jesus Christ— who became flesh and sends His Spirit to dwell within everyone who trusts in Him.

When we allow God to speak into our lives, we receive CRAZY HOPE and discover our TRUE IDENTITY. Take some time to immerse yourself in the truths found in the following pages, and allow the Holy Spirit to guide you and teach you about the truth of who you are in Christ. God wants to dispel the lies you believe and the darkness surrounding you so that His truth and light can set you free.

Let your CRAZY HOPE in Christ form your TRUE IDENTITY.

OUR IDENTITY IN CHRIST

WE HAVE...

- the hope of eternal life (Titus 3:7)

- the ministry of reconciliation (2 Cor. 5:18)

- the message of reconciliation (2 Cor. 5:19)

- Christ dwelling in our hearts (Eph. 3:17)

- access to the throne of God (Rom. 5:2, Eph. 3:12, Heb. 4:16)

- a heavenly home being prepared for us (John 14:1-2)

- an anchor for our soul (Heb. 6:19)

- authority over the power of the enemy (Luke 10:19)

- power to witness (Acts 1:8)

- peace with God (Rom. 5:1)

- a Father of compassion (2 Cor. 1:3)

- a God of all comfort (2 Cor. 1:3)

- a Savior who died for us (Rom. 5:8)

- a Sanctifier who lives within us (1 Cor. 1:30, Gal. 2:20)

- a Healer who restores us (James 5:15)

- a King who returns for us (Rev. 1:7; 19:16; 22:12)

- the Spirit who fills us (Eph. 5:18)

- the Spirit who guides us (John 16:13)

- the Spirit who gifts us (1 Cor. 12:4-11)

- the Spirit who bears His fruit through us (Gal. 5:22-23)

- a faith of greater worth than gold (1 Peter 1:7)

- an inheritance kept in heaven that can never perish, spoil, or fade (1 Peter 1:4)

- assurance of salvation (John 5:25, Rom. 8:16)

- great and precious promises (2 Peter 1:4)

- our names written in the book of life
  (Luke 10:20, Rev. 3:5; 21:27)

- everything we need for life (2 Peter 2:1)

- everything we need for godliness (2 Peter 2:1)

WE ARE...

- complete in Him (Col. 2:10)

- washed, sanctified, and justified (1 Cor. 6:11)

- set apart for the Master's use (2 Tim. 2:21)

- shielded by God's power (1 Peter 1:5)

- kept in His hand (John 10:29)

- kept from falling (Jude 1:24)

- kept by the power of God (1 Peter 1:5)

- not condemned (Rom. 8:1-2)

- one with the Lord (1 Cor. 6:17)

- strengthened by His mighty power (Eph. 3:16)

- seated in heavenly places (Eph. 1:3; 2:6)

- His very own people eager to do good (Titus 2:14)

- called with a holy calling (2 Tim. 1:9)

- greatly loved (Rom. 1:7, Eph. 2:4)

- protected from the evil one (2 Thess. 3:3, 1 John 5:18)

- equipped with spiritual armor (Eph. 6:10-18, 1 Thess. 5:8)

- the salt of the earth (Matt. 5:13)

- the light of the world (Matt. 5:14)

- born again (1 Peter 1:23)

- the Lord's servants (2 Tim. 2:24)

- a holy priesthood (1 Peter 2:5)

- a royal priesthood (1 Peter 2:9)

- a chosen people (1 Peter 2:9)

- a holy nation (1 Peter 2:9)

- a people belonging to God (1 Peter 2:9)

- aliens and strangers in this world (1 Peter 2:11)

- citizens of heaven (Phil. 3:20)

- assured that we will suffer for Him (2 Tim. 3:12)

- promised that we will reign with Him (2 Tim. 2:12)

- recipients of mercy (1 Peter 2:10)

- more than conquerors (Rom. 8:37)

- hidden with Christ in God (Col. 3:3)

- being transformed into His likeness (2 Cor. 3:18)

- We Are His (2 Tim. 2:19)[8]

---

[8] This type of list has been compiled by many others as well. This particular edition was assembled by John Stumbo and is available at https://www.cmalliance.org/about/family/leadership/download/Who-We-Are-In-Christ.pdf.

ABOUT THE AUTHOR

Dan is a licensed and ordained minister with the Christian and Missionary Alliance. As a writer and passionate speaker, Dan seeks to bring a message of hope to a hopeless world!

Dan considers 1989 his greatest year: graduation from high school, the birth of his firstborn son, becoming a Christian, marrying his high school sweetheart, and starting his first job.

Dan and his wife Kimberly have been together for over thirty years. Because of his injuries, physicians informed Dan that he would never be able to have children. However, God has blessed Dan and his wife with four children of their own and the privilege of adopting a fifth from the foster system. They are now blessed with seven grandchildren.

Made in the USA
Las Vegas, NV
03 March 2021